T0089166

Cambridge Elements ≡

Elements in Publishing and Book Culture
edited by
Samantha Rayner
University College London
Leah Tether
University of Bristol

EDITING FICTION

Three Case Studies from Post-war Australia

Alice Grundy
Australian National University

CAMBRIDGE
UNIVERSITY PRESS

CAMBRIDGE
UNIVERSITY PRESS

University Printing House, Cambridge CB2 8BS, United Kingdom

One Liberty Plaza, 20th Floor, New York, NY 10006, USA

477 Williamstown Road, Port Melbourne, VIC 3207, Australia

314–321, 3rd Floor, Plot 3, Splendor Forum, Jasola District Centre,
New Delhi – 110025, India

103 Penang Road, #05–06/07, Visioncrest Commercial, Singapore 238467

Cambridge University Press is part of the University of Cambridge.

It furthers the University's mission by disseminating knowledge in the pursuit of
education, learning, and research at the highest international levels of excellence.

www.cambridge.org
Information on this title: www.cambridge.org/9781009017794
DOI: 10.1017/9781009039383

First published 2022

A catalogue record for this publication is available from the British Library.

ISBN 978-1-009-01779-4 Paperback
ISSN 2514-8524 (online)
ISSN 2514-8516 (print)

Editing Fiction

Three Case Studies from Post-war Australia

Elements in Publishing and Book Culture

DOI: 10.1017/9781009039383
First published online: July 2022

Alice Grundy
Australian National University

Author for correspondence: Alice Grundy, alicektg@gmail.com

ABSTRACT: *Editing Fiction* considers the collaborative efforts of literary production as well as editorial practice in its own right, using case studies by Australian novelists Jessica Anderson, Thea Astley and Ruth Park. An emphasis on collaboration is necessary because literary criticism often takes books as finite, discrete works rather than the result of multiple contributors' labour, engaged to differing degrees. The editorial process always involves a negotiation over edits for the sake of the work, taking its potential reception or projected sales into account. Through examination of the archives, this Element shows that editing can be formative, limiting, commercially directed, a literary collaboration or a mix of all these interventions. For editors and scholars alike, the Element examines practices of the recent past, seeking to determine the responsibilities of editors and publishers to authors, to the text itself and to society, and the interrelation of editorial work, social conditions and market forces.

This Element also has a video abstract: www.cambridge.org/grundy

KEYWORDS: editing, publishing, book history, literary criticism, post-colonial studies

ISBNs: 9781009017794 (PB), 9781009039383 (OC)
ISSNs: 2514-8524 (online), 2514-8516 (print)

Contents

Introduction

> We always say our aim is to make each book the best conceivable version of itself, but we should add, *for its readers*.
>
> *(Brett, 2011: 79)*

During a podcast discussion with the author Anne Enright, the *New Yorker* fiction editor Deborah Triesman describes differences between a Frank O'Connor short story as published in that magazine and the version published in a collection decades later (2016). Triesman invites Enright to comment on the potential significance of changes to the characters' names. It is not the only time she has drawn attention to changes to a story from one version to the next, and notably, in a number of podcasts, Triesman has asked similar questions of other guests. This reflects the fact that as a longstanding fiction editor, one of her jobs is to develop stories for the magazine. At the same time, while she is happy to discuss variations in *published* texts, Triesman almost never discusses 'invisible' edits – that is to say, changes that are made *in advance of* publication – even though she has personally worked with many of the authors who feature on the podcast during the pre-publication stage.

The distinction made by Triesman between these two kinds of changes is noteworthy for research about publishing culture because it mirrors an important distinction between two kinds of editing, which I will call 'textual editing' and 'professional editing'. As used here, professional editing is the work undertaken in advance of publication when an editor works in collaboration with an author. This is the editing that Triesman enacts in her role as fiction editor; a role that can range from correcting typos to suggestions about plot, characterisation or setting. Textual editing, as used here, is concerned with changes made to a text – whether by an author, editor or in the course of production (for example, by a typesetter) – which become evident in the post-publication stage, when a scholar or critic compares a published edition with earlier versions of a work; for example, a late holograph or typescript.

In brief, while textual editing, sometimes called scholarly editing, is generally concerned with work already in the public record in some form, and happens after a book has been published, professional editing takes place pre-publication and is usually kept private and invisible.

The motives are different, too: textual editing is work carried out by scholars and critics interested in tracing changes in an author's vision: for example, work on Joyce and his many revisions of *Ulysses* (Sullivan, 2013). These are also the sorts of differences that Triesman discusses with guests, for example when an author changes a character's name between different published versions of a work. In some schools of scholarly editing, such as 'final-intentionalist editing' of the Greg-Bowers-Tanselle school (Sullivan, 2013: 9), the focus is on whether any 'corruptions' came between the authorial vision and the published work.

On the *New Yorker* podcast, Triesman regularly discusses changes to a work *between* editions but almost never reveals information about professional edits made as part of an initial preparation for publication.[1] And she is not alone: such edits are rarely discussed, in part because of the secrecy around professional editing, based on the commonly held notion that exposure of that kind could embarrass authors. Textual editing is a large and rich field of scholarship. Coverage of professional editing is scarce.

Nevertheless, professional editing makes a pronounced difference to published works. This Element, therefore, aims to demonstrate how consideration of professional editing can offer new perspectives on existing scholarship and our understanding of published work. It also affords students and junior editors a detailed insight into the kinds of processes at play and the possible ramifications of an infelicitous intervention. In each of the case studies here, the editing and publishing process impacts on the book in marked and at times surprising ways. By drawing carefully on archival sources to examine the editorial process and develop a picture of the changes to a text as it moves through multiple hands on the way to publication, I hope to demonstrate just how important the study of professional editing can be.

---

[1] In the episode where Andrew Sean Greer reads Dorothy Parker's 'I Live on Your Visits', Triesman mentions a revelation from Marion Meade's biography that Parker's editors requested the excision of a gay character from the story since her publishers, Simon & Schuster, were too prudish to publish it with such a character.

Editorial input is usually the work of a number of different individuals at different stages of production – sometimes before acquisition and invariably after. In some cases there are not complete records for the editorial process, but I have included as much detail as possible, especially in the interests of differentiating between the roles of different individuals in each book's passage from draft to published edition. The following terms are standard for differentiating types of editorial work:

– Structural editing, which involves consideration of elements such as plot, characterisation and setting;
– Copyediting, concerned with sentence structure, language and expression, as well as grammar, spelling and punctuation;
– Proofreading, which comes after the manuscript has been typeset, and includes checks for things such as typographical errors and the presentation of words on the page.

Naturally there is some crossover between the different stages, but I have attempted to be as clear as possible about which editor performed which role in each case.

I have said that coverage of professional editing is scarce. On the rare occasions it is discussed in print, it is usually in relation to three specific genres. The first is memoir, with famous examples including Diana Athill (2009) and Robert Gottlieb (2016), who recount their relationships with famous authors and their glamorous long lunches. The second place it can be found is in textbooks designed for tertiary editing courses (Einsohn and Schwartz, 2019; Mackenzie, 2011; Flann, Hill and Wang, 2014), and the third is the anthology of interviews or essays, directed at the tertiary education market and for those curious about the editing process (Ginna, 2017; Greenberg, 2015; Gross, 1993).

Recently, with growing attention to publishing studies and continued interest in the sociology of literature (English, 2010), coverage of professional editing is starting to increase. Two notable titles in the past few years have brought attention to this type of labour. The first is Susan Greenberg's *A Poetics of Editing* (2018). Drawing from personal experience as a professional editor, *Poetics of Editing* outlines ways of thinking about the editor as a bodily incarnation of an imagined reader. It posits that editing is a process of opening and closing, of considering multiple possibilities and versions before closing in on one version that then becomes public (246). The editor balances competing priorities of the imagined reader, the publisher's requirements and the author's desires, as well as determining which changes can be made to ensure the book becomes the best version of itself. While textual editing privileges the author's vision, often to the exclusion of other factors, professional editing balances the demands of the author's intentions with the publisher, the expected reader and their own judgement.

Secondly, *The Art of Editing* by Tim Groenland (2019) outlines the limitations of existing methodologies in recognising collaborative efforts in genetic criticism (13). As well as using genetic criticism for his methodological toolkit, Groenland finds useful material in Jerome McGann's work on textual criticism and his description of the 'socialization of texts' (1991). Groenland's analysis takes two author–editor relationships as its subject: the maximalism of David Foster Wallace and his posthumously published novel *The Pale King*, edited by Michael Pietsch, and the restrained minimalism of Raymond Carver's short stories, edited by Gordon Lish. Both are famously visible and highly interventionist examples at opposite ends of literary fashion in the twentieth century.

Like the work of Groenland, this Element uses genetic criticism but it includes material that has previously been unseen for the most part. Australia's most celebrated book editor, Beatrice Davis, spoke of the importance of 'invisible mending', as the contemporary Australian publisher Jane Palfreyman reminds readers (Cosic, 2016). This project takes work that has been private and brings it to light, not with the intention of undermining writers' works or their skill but to better understand the production of that work.

There is a question of ethics in the choice to discuss what had previously been private. Since each of the authors voluntarily contributed their drafts and correspondence to archives, often annotating their files to assist that process, it seems that they anticipated a researcher such as myself examining the texts. There is the additional ethical question about how an editor's work relates to 'communitarian interest and [how it] pursues cultural innovation and social equality' as Lawrence Venuti (2010: 79) characterises

Alain Badiou's thinking about the ethics of translation.[2] By examining the relationship between the suggested edits and questioning the motivation behind them, I will confront exactly this question.

My approach is underpinned by my experience as a professional editor in Australia[3] for more than a dozen years and the industry insight that brings. Unlike most writing on editing to date, this Element focuses on the kinds of edits that are common: that is to say, editorial intervention, which involves suggestions and comments with some noteworthy changes, but that stops well short of rewriting. For the most part, professional editing involves fewer and less radical changes than the work of Pietsch and Lish but, nevertheless, these amendments are significant and communicate important information about the aesthetic, social and commercial forces exerting influence on the editor, the text and the author.

There is an associated gender split between the subjects of existing study where the editor has reached a degree of fame: Gordon Lish, Michael Pietsch, Ezra Pound, Andrew Edward Garnett and Maxwell Perkins represent cases where the intervention could sometimes be described as rewriting; each of these editors is male, as is each of the authors with whom they famously collaborated. Aside from two separate books on female editors of 'little magazines' (Marek, 1995; Irvine, 2016), and one out of four case studies in Abram Foley's book *The Editor Function* that takes Chris Kraus and her feminist editing as its subject (2021), discussions of editing almost always focus on male examples. From Wayne Koestenbaum's *Double Talk* (1989) to Hannah Sullivan's *The Work of Revision* (2013) and Jack Stillinger's *Multiple Authorship and the Myth of Solitary Genius* (1991), when engaging with editing, the names that repeatedly surface are those I have already mentioned: Carver and Lish; Perkins and Wolfe; Eliot and Pound. These are all white men and all editors are highly interventionist. While Lish made changes to as much as 70 per cent of Carver's stories

---

[2] For more on similarities – and key differences – between editing and translation and in particular the invisibility of the project, see Greenberg, 2018: 43–4

[3] While Australia is a small market compared with the US and the UK, the processes and practices echo the work editors undertake in other English-speaking markets.

(Max, 1998), and Perkins worked for extended periods turning thousands of pages of draft into hundreds of pages of novel (Berg, 2013), most editorial labour does not have that level of impact on the published work. Perhaps it is in part because the work undertaken by female editors is usually not as drastic, it has not attracted the same attention from scholars; although, as the case studies in this Element demonstrate, even relatively minor interventions can lead to remarkable changes.

This observation about the gendered element of editorial labour is important because the contemporary industry is overwhelmingly staffed by women, and women are also the largest book-buying demographic (Wrathall, 2018; Throsby, Zwar and Morgan, 2017), In Australia, furthermore, two thirds of authors are female (Throsby et al., 2017). Such under-representation of female editors in a serious analysis of the practice therefore calls for redress.[4]

The first section will consider the role of the different readers in the acquisition and editing process, focusing on gatekeepers as first readers and their expectations of the reading public, and demonstrate the kinds of macro-level effects that influential parties such as funding bodies can have on a text. Here we look at *Swords and Crowns and Rings* (1977) by the Australian author Ruth Park, whose work has appeared on stage, on radio and in print for adults and children. Park has been a significant part of Australian culture in the twentieth century, winning literary awards as well as reaching readers with children's titles such as *The Muddleheaded Wombat*. The publishers of *Swords*, a long adult novel, wanted large cuts to the text in part because of the implications for accessing funding and in part because of concern about readers' responses to a short-statured protagonist.[5]

---

[4] Interestingly, there is more work on editing and race than editing and women. In the Australian context, literary scholars Adam Shoemaker (1989), Anita Heiss (2003), Penny van Toorn (2006), Jennifer Jones (2009) and Michele Grossman (2013) are prominent examples.

[5] In Australia the preferred term for people with skeletal dysplasia and other similar conditions is 'short-statured'. The novel and the contemporary criticism uses the word 'dwarf'.

The second section considers the editor's role as social barometer; for example, when querying an author's engagement with material from other cultures, and preparing the book for multiple territories or markets. *Multiple Effects of Rainshadow* (1996) was the penultimate book of one of Australia's most critically acclaimed authors, Thea Astley. Critics have cited *Multiple Effects*, her third work of fiction inspired by real events, as part of a trajectory of improved representation of Indigenous people across her career, and more broadly in the writing produced by settler authors over the second half of the twentieth century. In this study we see what the editor suggested and how those changes reveal information about the social norms of the time, complicating the scholarly debate about Astley's work.

The third section illustrates the differences in an author's responses to edits that expand and develop her idea of the work, and those that limit and inhibit it. In the case of Jessica Anderson's *Tirra Lirra by the River* (1978), the copyeditor's suggestions were problematic and Anderson asked for them to be 'cancelled', whereas a suggestion from her first publisher was a source of significant inspiration. These are real-world examples that counter 'the traditional perception of editing as the imposition of closure', as Greenberg (2018: vi) puts it; further, this example demonstrates that editing is 'a dynamic process with a built-in understanding of failure and a sense of the possible'.

Each of these cases comes from the second half of the twentieth century, since it was in this period that the industry saw a shift towards predominantly female editors. The same period witnessed the rise of second-wave feminism and a significant body of scholarship on women writers. The subjects – Ruth Park, Thea Astley and Jessica Anderson – are some of Australia's most celebrated authors: they each made a living from their writing; each won the Miles Franklin, Australia's most prestigious literary prize; and each has been studied at schools and universities since their books were first released. Each of their archives are rich and housed at some of Australia's premier cultural institutions and in each case multiple phases of the drafting and production process are extant. Naturally, an archive is not an uncontested space and the archives are not 'mere storehouses of records' but make for 'a significant element' of investigations, as archival scholars Dever, Newman and Vickery (2009: 10) put it.

Also important are the archival materials highlighted by genetic criticism – contemporaneous reviews, evidence about sources of inspiration and biographical details of the authors – which makes it a useful model for this project. Genetic criticism follows on from the work of Louis Hay (2004) as he describes the ways in which texts are in dialogue with, and informed by, the circumstances, impetus and component parts of their creation. As he puts it, 'To say that the text is marked by social structures, ideologies and cultural traditions is to say that it continues to speak to them, that in its warp and weft we can read, at every moment, the truth of the time' (23). Genetic criticism is interested both in the work itself and what the conditions of production describe about the time and situation in which it was created. This Element provides an example of the model by examining iterations of a given text, works that prompted the author or formed part of their research as well as responses after publication.

Perhaps the most relevant contribution from genetic criticism for this project is the work of Thomas Pynchon scholars Luc Herman and John M. Krafft. Their essay 'Fast Learner: The Typescript of Pynchon's *V.* at the Harry Ransom Center in Austin' employs genetic criticism to consider the author–editor dynamic and the effects of the interaction on a text. Importantly, they had access to the entirety of editor Corlies Smith's correspondence with Pynchon; this 'proved invaluable, since [the letters] provide the key to the connection between the Ransom Center's typescript and the published novel' (Herman and Krafft, 2007: 2). According to Herman and Krafft:

> the many substantial cuts do warrant further detailed examination, not just for their technical but also for their ideological dimension. We are thinking, for example, of the reduction of McClintic Sphere, and of the cuts relating to the theme of marriage. This work to come will deepen, complicate, and perhaps correct the image of Pynchon some readers have derived from the published works. *(18)*

The model that Krafft and Herman develop affords a better understanding of elements of the text. By reference to the changes that the manuscript underwent during the progression from holograph to printed book, a scholar can answer questions about the ideological and sociological underpinnings of a text and the ways in which the writer communicates these ideas, as well as what effects the editorial changes had on the work. In the case of the Pynchon archives, Krafft and Herman went on to write further articles considering elements such as race. Through analysis of the construction of Sphere as well as investigations of representations of gender and race (Krafft and Herman, 2015; 2018), their work shows the ways in which such archival mining yields rich critical results.

Through careful comparisons of the published works, and analysis of the changes made at different stages of the publishing process in the second half of the twentieth century, this Element offers unparalleled insight into the editing of fiction and the different kinds of social, economic, personal and aesthetic processes through which manuscripts progress *en route* to the reader. While Treisman may shy away from discussing edits in which she was involved, all the authors covered here have given their archives to libraries, seemingly with the expectation of researchers taking an interest in the means of production of their work. None of the authors are still alive and so I am reliant on written records, and vulnerable to whatever short-comings they may introduce. However, these resources are rich and, for the most part, have not been examined by scholars before now, especially in relation to the work of editors. This study uncovers surprising details from the archive contributing both to the textual record and the sociology of publishing in the second half of the twentieth century, a period of extra-ordinary change in terms of gender roles, race relations and economics. Without recognition of these influences and the associated role of the editing process, literary scholarship can only reach a limited understanding of a given text; and without the knowledge of editing history, contemporary editors may be condemned to repeat the mistakes of the past.

1 Editing and the Markets: Representation in Ruth Park's *Swords and Crowns and Rings*

Introduction

When we think of the reasons a novel might be significantly trimmed in the editorial process, we could suppose it is edited to make it more commercial: for example, by deletions of purple prose or to cut excessive exposition or 'telling'. What the present study shows is that other forces have unintended impacts on the editorial process that can be just as significant as aesthetic or commercial factors.

This chapter considers the novel *Swords and Crowns and Rings* by Ruth Park, an award-winning author of novels, books for children and young adults, radio plays and memoirs. When *Swords* was edited in 1977, interventions were not simply questions of aesthetics or readiness for the market; they were also determined by the requirement of a literary funding body to bring the work under a particular word length. The chapter also considers other suggested edits and their significance in the context of the novel and Park's oeuvre more broadly, as well as the implications of all such findings for an understanding of professional editing. Lastly, the archive material shared here demonstrates how resistance to editorial work can speak loudly about the author's intentions and expectations. To incorporate this dynamic into existing understandings of editorial work, I describe and then interrogate the forces that influence editorial intervention. By carefully considering the role of these mechanisms in the case of *Swords*, I demonstrate the importance of evaluating different editorial interventions in the publishing process, including when these forces are not embodied agents in the form of editors. I also show how combining attention to authorial impulses with attention to the drivers influencing editors and publishers involved in the book generates a richer understanding of the work.

A related point arises concerning differing expectations of the reader, and how this influences the attitudes author and editor have to the work, and therefore to the changes the author is prepared to make. The ways in which an expected reader is constructed are contingent on the circumstances and experiences of both editor and author, and we can see the effects of these influences in the edits and in Park's responses to the marked-up typescript.

This chapter also considers how editors as gatekeepers can perpetuate existing biases or limit representations of marginalised groups through the publication of works that reinforce those ideas. By considering the correspondence between Park and her editor and examining the edited typescript, we can see that Park had envisioned more open-minded readers and was also working to encourage a more accepting response to people with disability. In fact, her prose in some ways prefigured calls for rounded characters rather than what disability studies scholars David Mitchell and Sharon Snyder call 'narrative prosthesis' – defined as using disability as 'a stock feature of characterization and an opportunistic metaphorical device'. As these authors argue, such an approach produces 'a conundrum: while stories rely upon the potency of disability as a symbolic fixture, they rarely take up disability as experience of social or political dimensions' (Mitchell and Snyder, 2013: 222). In *Swords*, the protagonist's disability is not simply a plot device or a figurative element. The social, political and personal repercussions of his disability are questions that the book addresses directly, and Park's novel both explicitly and implicitly works to construct a fully realised character who is short-statured.

There were a number of different editors involved in the production of Park's novel. The majority of her correspondence was with Beatrice Davis, who was also responsible for the edit that can be seen as a structural edit/copy-edit hybrid. Davis would have been uncomfortable with the attention this chapter gives her editorial labour, since she, like other editors, believed she should be invisible. The work was acquired by publishing director Bob Sessions and the archive shows discussions with editor Sue Ebury, who was part of the acquisitions decision-making process. The archive does not include the proofread typescript, although it is highly likely the publisher, Thomas Nelson, engaged such an editor to prepare the novel for publication.

Of Australia's notable authors of the twentieth century, Ruth Park is one of the most prolific, having written across a range of genres and media, and her work has had a huge cultural impact through stage and screen adaptations of her novels, keeping her books continuously in print. Park is remembered in particular for her *Harp in the South* novels, the first of which won a *Sydney Morning Herald* prize and created a scandal that the paper played up for publicity (MLMSS 8075, Box 5, Folder 4). She came to Australia as a young woman, having already worked as a journalist in Auckland. Although she had a job offer from a newspaper, on discovering the tenor of its coverage, Park resigned and opted to freelance for many years to come (Park, 2019a). It is impossible write about her life without mentioning her Australian husband, novelist and journalist D'Arcy Niland. But unlike other spouses of famed authors, Niland made next to no creative contribution to his wife's work. He did not read novels very often and did not make an exception for his wife: as Park (2019b: 162) said in her memoir, 'He was never to read one of mine'. Park, however, did read all of Niland's writing, and despite the fact that she brought in as much money from her pen, if not more, it was Niland who had the desk in their house for many years while she worked from the kitchen table or ironing board (145).

The focus of this chapter follows Park's drafting of a short-statured character in one of her novels for adults and the responses of her prospective publishers to his disability. *Swords* is a coming-of-age story of Jackie, born short-statured, and his childhood playmate and later sweetheart, Dorothy 'Cushie' Moy, who live in the fictional town of Kingsland. Predominantly written in a realist mode, *Swords* also 'draws upon the ancient legends and fairy tales of Europe to tell the story of Australia' (Greaves, 1996: 149). When Jackie is unable to get a job after leaving school because of prejudice towards his disability, he moves north to help some relations, the Linz family, on their farm. After Jackie leaves home, Cushie finds she is pregnant with his child and moves to Sydney to stay with her aunt and arrange an abortion. Away from her comfortable home life, and depressed at her separation from Jackie, Cushie becomes an alcoholic before finding purpose by helping her grandmother run a charity. Meanwhile, during his stay with the Linzes, Jackie is abused and tormented and ultimately tricked into marrying his cousin, Maida. Marriage offers a new start, and Jackie creates a life with his wife away from the Linz family. Just as Jackie has found work and is hopeful for a future with his wife and small child, tragedy strikes and Maida and the baby are killed in a fire. Jackie is falsely accused of causing their deaths but is cleared by the coroner and returns to Kingsland. By now, the Depression has started, and it is even more difficult for him to find work. He travels with his stepfather, 'the Nun', from town to town, trying to survive. It is during these travels that Jackie's political thinking finds form and Park's commentary on economic policy and the suffering of working people emerges. Ultimately, after much hardship, Jackie and Cushie are reunited and plan to spend the rest of their lives together.

An Unlikely Partnership

When Park first encountered the woman who was to be the editor of several of her adult novels, it was an inauspicious start. Prestigious local publisher Angus & Robertson had agreed to publish her novel as the prize for winning a *Sydney Morning Herald* competition in 1948. Corresponding with the author for the first time, editor Beatrice Davis wrote that *The Harp in the South* was 'not the kind of book A & R cares to publish but we have a gentleman's agreement with the *Herald*' (Park, 2019b: 178). The tone, however, changes markedly over the course of their relationship.

In the biography *A Certain Style: Beatrice Davis, a Literary Life*, Jacqueline Kent, herself a professional editor for trade publishers, says that when Davis

> went to work for Thomas Nelson in 1973, Park followed her. Beatrice edited her novel *Swords and Crowns and Rings* (1977) – it won the Miles Franklin Award . . . – and *Missus*, about the early lives of characters from *The Harp in the South*. Beatrice also edited *Playing Beattie Bow*, which was published in 1980. After thirty-six years, then, her editorial relationship with Ruth Park returned to its beginnings, with a novel for children. *(Kent, 2002: 142)*

Notably, Kent emphasises the length of their relationship, the range of titles on which they worked together and the fact that the relationship ended on a positive note, with the hugely successful young adult book *Playing Beattie Bow*. This telling focuses on the connections, and not the ruptures in the relationship, which I will return to later in the chapter. It also skims over the difficulties Park had in finding a publisher before the book was acquired by Thomas Nelson.

What the archive shows is a slightly more complicated series of events that led to the continuation of Davis and Park's editorial relationship. In an internal note at Thomas Nelson, editor Sue Ebury wrote to Anne Godden and Beatrice Davis:

> Collins, Macmillans, A&R and Penguin have all rejected it. Collins weren't mad about the dwarf theme, and wanted to cut it severely, (author wouldn't consent); I'm not sure what A&R thought; John Hocker would have loved to do an original Penguin, but decided that it wasn't quite up to the literary standards required by that; Macmillans couldn't come at the main character being a dwarf – turned them right off! The idea turned me off too, but I overcame the feeling quite quickly. *(MLMSS 7638, Folder 12)*

While Ebury may have hesitated initially, Nelson moved to contract the novel so long as the author agreed to certain conditions. Although Davis was a contractor for Thomas Nelson in the late 1970s, not a staff member, and normally an offer of publication comes from a company employee, she was the person who wrote to Park with an offer. She said the book was

> a wonderful piece of work which Nelson's would very much like to publish – <u>if</u> you can bring yourself to agree to cutting by about 30,000 words. I do pray that you can – whether you do this yourself or allow me to suggest how and where. It would be wonderful to be working with you again after so many years. *(MLMSS 7638/12, BD to RP, 13 August 1976)*

It is not uncommon for publishers to stipulate terms when agreeing to publish a work; however, it is less common for those terms to be determined, even in part, by a bureaucratic body. In the case of *Swords*, one of the determinations was the cultural and financial force of Literature Board grants.

In an internal letter from Thomas Nelson publisher Robert Sessions to editor Beatrice Davis, he wrote:

> The 30,000 words which we asked to be cut is simply a figure which brings the total word length within the ambit of the maximum grant available from the Literature Board. The grant is sufficient for us to be able to go over the maximum number of words if we absolutely have to and this figure is probably no more than a useful yardstick ... Quite frankly, whatever can be cut will help the costing enormously and I believe will also improve the book. However, I do not want to fall out with Ruth over, say, 5,000 words here or there. *(MLMSS 7638/12, RS to BD, 18 November 1976)*

If the grant only covers a certain word length, then anything over that amount would be more expensive for the publisher to produce; Sessions is saying that for each few thousand words over the limit, the book will have a smaller profit margin. He softens his request with a comment that he also does not want to ruin the relationship with Park, since he would have understood that it is in large part an author's cooperative efforts that help sell a book once it becomes available. Beside which – as Nelson's continued publishing of Park demonstrates – they were interested in continuing the relationship. The fact that he drew on a publishing truism by saying a trim would improve the book suggests that he was trying to soften the blow by offering a common rationale.

Park asked:

> Who fixed this arbitrary figure and why? Longer novels are more and more being published. Taking at random two from my shelf, I have counted them up ... Margaret Drabble's *Needle's Eye* is almost 163,000, and it covers a very small area of time, space, life. Kerryn Jones's *Holding On* is over 150,000, though that covers a longish lifetime and is a spacious book in character development and historical happening.

Please answer this question.
(MLMSS 7638/12, RP to BD, 10 November 1976)

The archive does not include a straightforward response from Davis on the question of the word length, although of course it does not mean that no answer was offered. Perhaps it was a mistake on the part of the publisher to mention a particular number of words that needed to be removed rather than to talk of the kinds of material to be taken out, since that would likely have been more persuasive from an artistic perspective. But the fact remains that word count seems arbitrary because it is: a number determined by bureaucrats at the Literature Board rather than the marketplace (as evidenced by Ruth Park's reference to books of similar lengths on her bookshelf) or according to the internal logic of the novel itself.

In response to Davis's request that Park make significant cuts, she continued:

> Yes, I am willing to do cuts, provided they are in keeping with my overall plan for the novel. I worked terribly hard on its shape, I think I have achieved harmony and balance, and I do not want to do anything to interfere with this.
>
> Thirty thousand is an awful whack to come out of a closely-planned [sic] novel, and at the moment the idea frightens me.
>
> However, you know I have intimate knowledge of your literary judgement, and I would welcome hearing what cuts you think would be good ones.
>
> *(MLMSS 7638/12, RP to BD, 19 August 1976)*

Park is taking part in the delicate dance between author and editor here, flattering her editor while also holding her position on the question of cutting out material that was the product of careful work and development. Park had produced many drafts, investing time in research and planning to produce the novel, and was not prepared to change it without good reason. Later in the same letter, Park added, 'You will infer from the above that any cuts to be made, if they are to be, I should do myself' (MLMSS 7638/12, RP to BD, 19 August 1976).

The covering letter that accompanied the edited typescript is of note because of the picture it paints about the editorial relationship. In a traditional editorial manoeuvre, Davis flattered Park, debased herself and then shifted some of the responsibility on to the publisher and the exigencies of the marketplace, writing: 'I enjoyed reading the story again, but felt both timid and impertinent in suggesting the cutting of such a sound and well-structured piece of work – to achieve what I've been told is necessary for those dull, practical reasons' (MLMSS 7638/12, BD to RP, 3 November 1976). Her word choice, in particular 'timid and impertinent', clearly positions her below the author and softens what might otherwise be perceived as a kind of slight on Park's artistic prowess. Davis also manages to skirt the potential comment that the book would benefit from being trimmed out of consideration for style or content by saying that she must suggest deletions for 'dull, practical reasons'.

In responding to the edit, at the start of the letter Park says she's glad Davis provided her home address so she could write a more frank response.

> Forgive me, I had forgotten, temporarily, that you are a true workman. But I have recalled it all over again. Most of your cuts I accept without question. Some I shall replace by others of the same length.
> *(MLMSS 7638/12, RP to BD, 10 November 1976)*

Park would have had more motivation to meet the condition of editing the manuscript because she did not have other offers from other publishers, but she also expressed pleasure at the prospect of being edited by Davis again, writing: 'I have always known that, like a good Greek actor "you do not put yourself above your poet". And whatever my faults and frailties as a writer – which I do most deeply realise – I do also have the good Greek actor's profound feeling … "You do not put yourself above the god." Which is truth' (MLMSS 7638/12, RP to BD, 10 November 1976). Park is outlining a clear hierarchy here as she compares herself with the Greek poet; the actor is Davis's avatar with 'truth' sitting at the top. This comparison with another art form also flags Park's understanding that this sort of collaborative process is a reality in different kinds of art. Park concludes the point by saying, 'I think that whatever way I have had success as a writer ... and the only success I prize at all is that readers <u>recognise</u> my characters ... is because I have tried to be true to the god.' As the linchpin for her argument as to why she wants to maintain certain material and is unprepared to accept trims on it, Park invokes the imagined reader and her sense of how they value her work.

When Greenberg figures the editorial relationship in her *Poetics of Editing*, there is no hierarchy, although there is an equivalent delineation between author, editor and work as she maps her schema onto Edmund Burke's triangulation of 'Spoken-to', 'Speech' and 'Speaker'. Park's invocation of the relationship is in the context of the 'good Greek actor' wanting to emphasise that Park will only act according to what she sees as the 'God' in this context: truth. I take Park to use truth in a broad sense of the term, meaning things that are true about the human condition. Further, Park identifies her fidelity to this God as the source of the success that she values most highly, readers' responses. What is equivalent in the two characterisations is a dynamic process of working through the creative material with an end goal of developing the text.

While many authors may tacitly consider such a question, it is useful to have Park's expression of the dynamic, especially in her response to Davis's edit. One reading of her articulation is that Park wants to affirm her position in the hierarchy and to legitimise her decision to stet Davis's edits, in particular in relation to character. As we will see in the following section, the cuts to a character that Park resisted the most were those relating to her short-statured protagonist, Jackie Hanna.

Taking a Risk

One type of editorial change that Park resisted most strongly was that which concerned her protagonist, Jackie; specifically, trims that removed references to his short stature and the impact this had on his experience of the world. Since Park accepted other edits, in particular relating to peripheral characters, the places where she stood firm are notable. Further, in a letter to Davis, Park emphasises the importance of keeping the descriptions of Jackie and his experiences:

> I must keep in material about dwarfs, how they are the same as other people, just smaller . . . and how greedily they grab any information about historic dwarfs which shows that a man's stature does not matter. And I must, even if I do it in a briefer way, give anecdotes which show the really terrible condition of Australia, particularly in New South Wales, during the Depression.
>
> *(MLMSS 7638/12, RP to BD, 10 November 1976)*

Park writes of Jackie 'greedily grabbing' stories of short-statured characters early on in the book.[6] Jackie shows Cushie picture books of 'black elves working at their goldsmiths' forges', and together they go into the hills in search of 'a whole race of people' like him (Park, 2012: 15). Around the time that *Swords* was published, there were other short-statured characters in Australian literature, such as in Park's earlier novel *Pink Flannel* (1955) and Christopher Koch's *The Year of Living Dangerously* (1979), but there had not yet been a book with a protagonist disabled in this way.[7]

Turning to the edited typescript and edits connected to the representation of disability, there is a note from Davis in the margin of one page, asking, 'Ruth, could you delete this episode.' The episode in question is where Jackie remembers his attempt to get a job in the office at the Dairy Co-op and the interviewer tries to dissuade him on the grounds of Jackie's 'delicate health' (MLMSS 8075/4/4: 113). Park's response was short, emphatic, written in red and circled: 'No.'

---

[6] While there is no record in the archive of Park interviewing short-statured people (although there is a record of Park interviewing someone about the Depression (MLMSS 8727/2/5)), she mentions such research in two separate newspaper interviews (Jordan, 1978: 37; Riddell, 1977: 8).

[7] Perhaps Thea Astley's *The Acolyte* (1972) comes the closest with a major character who is blind, but disabled protagonists were not something that had figured in Australian literature to that point.

Davis also suggests cutting an episode later in the text when Jackie is trying to improve his situation and get a job as a bookkeeper. After initial rejection Jackie says to his prospective employer: 'I'm a good bookkeeper sir, and you don't need height for that.' In response: 'The man stared, his pulpy face swelling with blood pressure or affront. Jack thought: He's in a funk for his own job. If he takes on a dwarf there'll be someone after his hide and he can't risk it' (723). The episode is important because it shows that Jackie, despite all the discrimination that he faces, still has empathy for someone in a difficult position. This generosity of spirit sets him apart from other characters and elevates him.

Elsewhere, Davis suggests a cut when Jackie asks a Catholic priest for a student's uniform as a way to replace some of his tattered clothes. The priest stares at Jackie's body as he is getting changed, and Jackie says, 'Picture, aren't I?' (721). None of these instances of suggested edits in relation to short stature are connected to mythic representations of 'dwarfs', and none are crucial to the plot, qualities that would risk a kind of narrative prosthesis. Through these scenes, Park is emphasising Jackie's experiences in the world in which he finds barriers where others would face no difficulty. Each case actively avoids 'narrative prosthesis' by showing Jackie as a flesh-and-blood character who is navigating professional and personal circumstances. Jackie ultimately passes many of the milestones that might be considered notable in an 'ordinary' life: he is gainfully employed, finds love (first with Cushie, then with Maida, then Cushie again), fathers a child and is politically and socially engaged.

Aside from stetting the scenes with the interviewers and priest, Park also resisted cuts of realist sections in the novel with descriptions of the 'orthopaedic and optical deterioration' (48–9) that Jackie learns could be a difficulty for him in the future, as associated effects of reduced growth. Park again resists cuts of similar material a little later in the manuscript (97).

Where Park did accept edits are those occasions where Jackie was figured in a mythic way, suggesting that she was actively refining the characterisation. For instance, Davis suggested trimming a description of Jackie daydreaming about people like him: 'No dwarfs lived there, nor amongst the haystacks of festering timber where towers and windlasses had collapsed, filling the tainted scrub with snakepits of corroded wire rope' (33).

Park's fairy-tale characterisation of short-statured people in this sequence renders them less realistic characters, less fully formed and persuasive and more tools for metaphor and imagery.

For the most part, Park works to avoid the kind of one-dimensional characterisation that attracts the charge of narrative prosthesis. Not only is the reader told about his search for work and his engagement with economic theory, we also see his romantic interests with repeated depictions of Jackie as a sexual character with desires, who finds pleasure with Cushie (54) and Maida (222). These scenes clearly place Jackie as a rounded human character and not a mythic or fairy-tale presence in the novel. As Park was keen to emphasise in her letter to Davis, characterisation was what she considered the strongest aspect of her writing, and by insisting on the inclusion of scenes explicitly relating to Jackie's short stature we can recognise that she saw this material as key to the project of the novel.

The Product of Careful Research

Another significant series of cuts to which Park objected concerned her depiction of the Depression. For instance, Davis suggested a substantive trim at the start of section V, 'Jackie Hanna 1931' (MLMSS 8075/4/4: 513–30), where there are descriptions of camps, itinerant workers and hardships. Davis suggested significant cuts to material about 'hobos' and their living conditions (523), as well as descriptions of men's faces and their missing teeth (530). However, Park elected to keep the majority of this material in the finished work, even though it was not crucial to the plot. As we know from her note to Davis, it was important to her to keep the material relating to the Depression: 'I must, even if I do it in a briefer way, give anecdotes which show the really terrible condition of Australians, particularly in New South Wales, during the Depression' (MLMSS 7638/12, RP to BD, 10 November 1976). In another instance, Davis made a suggestion to cut material related to the 'Interest on the British Bonds' (MLMSS 8075/4/4: 688). This relates to the exorbitant loan repayments that Australia owed England following the First World War and the debate that was under way in Australia at the time about whether or not to default on the loans when local people were starving. Rejecting these kinds of edits fits with Park's determination to preserve the historical record.

Park's archives hold newspaper clippings, notes from interviews and notes from books that she read as she researched the project (MLMSS 8727/2/5). That she included this research with the papers as part of the collection at the library marks her desire for future scholars to understand the depth of her work, even though some elements were drawn from her own life.[8]

The decision to keep her research for the archive can be read as a comment on the seriousness with which she approached the task of writing historical fiction. It is not a coincidence that the file for research on *Swords* is a thick one and that she included it with the material she gave to the Mitchell Library. Her notes on interviews, responses to newspaper stories of the day and details garnered from books demonstrate her meticulous approach and show that she wanted anyone who consulted the archive to be able to retrace her steps.

As with the proposed edits to the material about Jackie and his short stature, we can see that the suggested trims to material about the Depression reflect a different sensibility in relation to the work and the author's ends than those of the editor. Park was making social and political commentary and was using her research and personal experience of the Depression to comment on conditions of that period, in an attempt to educate an audience that may not have been alive at the time and to interrogate how governments weigh the immediate needs of their constituents against more abstract policy questions such as interest repayments on loans.

The painstaking effort that Park made in terms of interviews, archival research and getting details right was recognised by the eminent Australian historian Manning Clark in a letter that he wrote to her following the book's release. He enthused:

[8] To take one example, in her memoir *A Fence Around the Cuckoo*, Park (2019a: 38) tells the story of her father seeing a destitute carpenter's belongings sold at auction. Her father bought the man's tool kit to return to him – an incident that she later used in *Swords*.

You have that gift to tell a story, which [is] the envy of every
writer, [including?] Myself, who tries to write history as
a story. You also have the GRACE to be able to look at
people in the 'LOWER DEPTHS' of life and confer on
them a sensibility and aesthetic grandeur.

Permit me also to thank you for publishing one to understand Australians – being so say [?] for why we are as we
are. *(MLMSS 8555/4/2, MC to RP, 15 January 1978)*

In a copy of her response that Park kept, she wrote, 'I conclude that to
me [history] is merely a long succession of "nows". Its fascination for me is
because through its study I can see and assess how a brief "now" in 1910 was
the seed of a series of other "nows" which coalesced in many of the nows of
today' (MLMSS 8555/4/2). Park wanted to communicate the reality of
these 'many nows' to her reader by including anecdotes about the extra-
ordinary poverty of the Depression, and her resistance to cuts of this
material, despite the conditional offer of publication, emphasises the importance of history to Park's conception of the text.

Without the insight of the archive, and knowledge of Park's resistance to
these changes, we would not understand her intentions for the work, and we
would not have the understanding of the kinds of pressures that the
publisher was negotiating simultaneously. By using the information we
gain from genetic criticism and from studying the professional editing and
publishing history of the work, we can assess both Park's vision and where
that conflicted with the expectations of her editor and publisher.

Mr Moy

One of the changes from the edit of greatest interest to this project comes
from Beatrice Davis's excision of material about, or from the perspective of,
Cushie's dad Mr Moy. Unlike the suggested cuts to material about Jackie's
short stature or the Depression, Park acquiesced to Davis's trims of this
character. In the draft that Park first submitted, Mr Moy was a more
prominent character, with material written from his perspective in close
third person. The published novel, however, has a clear demarcation

between the overwhelmingly male 'Jackie' sections and the female 'Cushie' sections in which Mr Moy makes only very limited appearances.

The reader is first introduced to Mr Moy at the start of the book as having a 'rare moment of humour' when he said his daughter looked just like a little cushion, an observation soon shortened to 'Cushie' (Park, 2012: 12). We soon learn that although Cushie 'idolised her handsome father', for her mother Mr Moy was 'the cause of her exile from riches and admiration' (13). His financial position is again the focus of his characterisation at the next appearance, when we discover that he 'frequently found himself with a bitter taste in his mouth. He was jealous' (59). This description comes just before one of the first significant cuts to his presence in the book:

> Cushie, in her new, strangely smelling black clothes, looked dignified and very Saxon, a real Jackaman for which Mr Moy was thankful. If only James, the old devil, had seen her before he died, her legacy would be more certain. But surely – his own granddaughter! And Isobel had been prevailed upon to send photographs of the girls to their grandmother at least once a year. There was no need to worry, surely. *(MLMSS 8075/4/4: 110)*[9]

We see a number of ideas from Mr Moy's perspective here, including his final conclusion that he should not worry. His reflections on Cushie's 'Saxon' appearance are also relevant in terms of the religious affiliations of the characters, a point to which I will return.

By cutting some of the interiority that helps the reader develop a richer understanding of Mr Moy, the edit shifts his characterisation and his role in the text and leaves him as a plot device rather than a convincing human presence. Without his thoughts, Mr Moy is much more distant and has a far smaller role in the text.

It was not just Mr Moy's interiority that was cut but also comments on his agency (or lack thereof):

---

[9] This excision was pencilled in the margin, and then Park agreed to the cut.

> But of course Cushie was ~~strapped, not by her father, who~~
> ~~came of a class that never raised a hand to a female, but by~~
> ~~her mother. Hopping, shrieking, promising never to go to~~
> ~~the hills again, she was~~ whacked ~~at~~ [by her mother] all the
> way up the stairs into her room. *(MLMSS 8075/4/4: 39)*

Davis marked this edit in pen, without a pencil mark in the margin,
indicating that she intended it as a definite cut rather than the pencilled
suggestions elsewhere on the typescript.

Later, there is another significant Davis cut to the text. The original
passage read:

> Mr Moy flushed darkly. But what was he to say? He could
> offer no alternative way out of this catastrophe. Keep the
> whole matter dark as the grave, get rid of the – the thing, for
> he could not bring himself to think of it as his grandchild –
> keep Cushie in Sydney for a few weeks until she had
> recovered her health, and then forget all about it.
>
> *(MLMSS 8075/4/4: 298)*

Park agreed to remove all but the first sentence: as with the last example,
this text was exclusively the thoughts of Mr Moy. Again, on page 672, two
full paragraphs are struck through (marked in the margin and then deleted
by Park). These cuts underscore the point that there was a consistent and
intentional trimming of Mr Moy. Notably, such edits take place not only in
a given part of the book but all the way through, including an extended
section on pages 672–3. One reason these edits are important is because they
focus the Cushie sections of the book and, as stated earlier, give greater
emphasis to the duality of the male and female sections. The closest
analogue in the text for Mr Moy is Mrs Hanna, Jackie's mother (a parent
who is the opposite gender to the protagonist of the current section). Again,
there are no consistent and sustained cuts to her interiority. The reader
spends some time in the early sections following Mrs Hanna's responses to
Jackie's short stature (MLMSS 8075/4/4: 12–13). Davis did mark up some
potential extensive excisions around these sections, but they were pencilled

margin suggestions as opposed to pen strike-throughs, as in the case of the passages relating to Mr Moy. Park did not accept them. A few pages later, there is a cut to one sentence in a paragraph of Mrs Hanna's thoughts (42). This is a much smaller trim than equivalent material for Mr Moy. Similarly, there are parts that Davis could have cut concerning Mrs Moy (e.g. 85) but again, these were only marked with pencil in the margin and not approved by Park.

After careful consideration of the whole typescript, it is my contention that the treatment of Mr Moy is unique. If the primary aim of Davis's editorial work was to shorten the book overall, simplifying some of the side characters is a relatively light-handed way of achieving this. However, it is not something that Davis suggested for other secondary characters in the Cushie section who were female. Take, for example, Cushie's Aunt Claudie and her friend Iris. Although these characters are not central protagonists of the story, there are hardly any cuts, and none as long as a paragraph. It points to the unusual nature of the Mr Moy cuts, since they are the only edits of their kind. In reflecting on the material that Park consented to cutting, we see that Mr Moy as a male and one of the few Protestant characters in the work is not central to Park's vision for the novel. Paying attention to what was removed contributes to our understanding of what was central to Park's project.

Missus

Research about editing usually examines authors and their acceptance of editorial changes, and describes the importance of those interventions. However, editors are taught that the published text is always ultimately the product and responsibility of the author. The question then arises: what happens when there is a disagreement? How are such differences resolved, especially when the author is under pressure given limited options of publication? Of all the authors considered in this Element, Park had the longest-running relationship with her editor, but just as it did not start on good terms, the ending of their relationship was also fraught. With the last book came a falling out that was the product of a difference in sensibility and in expectations for the work, particularly the prose that the author used.

The archive holds evidence of the rupture in their relationship. That final book was the conclusion of the *Harp in the South* trilogy. This disagreement is perhaps not surprising given the fact that *Missus* is part of the same world as *Harp in the South*, the book that Davis had initially described as being unfit for Angus & Robertson.

In her edit, Davis argued that the tone of the *Missus* manuscript was too clipped and journalistic; for instance, when discussing Chapter Six in her queries, Davis wrote: 'The almost telegraphic manner doesn't give the reader a chance to savour, or even to assimilate, the significance of the action and reaction of the characters' (MLMSS 7638/13).

In an internal note to Robert Sessions at Nelson, Davis wrote, 'The MS. Will need quite a lot of work to make it popular and to avoid nasty reviews: it will get no literary acclaim. I'll do my utmost with tact and persuasion in talking to Ruth' (MLMSS 7638/13, BD to RS, 13 September 1984). Notable in her comment is Davis's invocation both of commercial and literary measures of success, that is, she says that without her edits the book would suffer both in terms of finding readers and in terms of critical responses.

True to form, when it came to delivering feedback to Park, Davis adopted many of the common editorial postures of subservience to the author and the work and personal fallibility, saying:

> And of course I feel nervous and embarrassed to be suggest-
> ing even small changes to a writer like you. Every spot of
> green ink I've put on the typescript seems an impertinence:
> and I hope you won't be angry with me and will believe that
> the suggested amendments are made with the very best of
> intentions. *(MLMSS 7638/13, BD to RP 19 October 1984)*

Contradicting the cover note, some of the suggestions marked on the typescript were rather strongly worded. For instance, in Chapter Nine, Davis's first query was: 'This chapter seems to [sic] scrappy and weak – though I like its comic ending. Could you please rethink it to make a more satisfying ending to this remarkable novel?' (MLMSS 7638/13, undated). In turn, Park's response was that she knows her readers well, another invocation of her anticipated audience, and that she has faith in her own talents.

In Park's archive, held at the Mitchell Library in Sydney, Park included a note from the time of the edits, discussing her internal debate over how to respond. The note is significant not just for its revelation of Park's state of mind but also for the fact that its inclusion in the archive demonstrates that Park desired for researchers to consider her responses to the edits and to have an insight into her thoughts on the author–editor relationship. Park writes:

> I cannot choose between a friend and a novel, the novel must win every time.
>
> I shall withdraw this novel rather than muck it about. There's no question and no indecision about that. I'm wondering, though, whether I shd ring Tim and tell him to hold the advance cheque, don't cash it, in case it has to go back . . .
>
> How to write that letter however? How to be kind? My experience is that people never accept rebuffs of this nature in the spirit in which they are offered.
>
> *(MLMSS 8078/5/Missus: undated)*

Park is so serious about these edits, she considers calling her agent to ask him to 'hold the advance', not wanting to accept money for the work; very likely because it would make her beholden to the publisher. After her internal wrestling, Park still wants to preserve what she can of her relationship with Davis, and in a letter explains:

> I fear that when you look again at this typescript you will be offended or hurt at the many deletions and measures of your editorial marks. You know how I cherish you. Truly I do not want to cause you vexation of any kind. But I cannot see eye to eye with you on the majority of these alterations.
>
> *(MLMSS 7638/13, RP to BD, 18 November 1984)*

Just as Davis tried to soften her responses with language, so Park tries to appease Davis, reminding her, 'You know how I cherish you.' There is an attempt here to separate the editor from the edits in her comment; this differs from prior correspondence, quoted earlier in this chapter, where there had been extensive emphasis on the personhood of Davis, and that it was her in particular who was engaged in the project.

Fitting with other expressions of her subservience to the author and their work, when Davis sent the (largely unchanged) pages to Robert Sessions she wrote: 'Ruth rejected many of my suggestions, and I don't blame her a bit. After all, she is the writer' (MLMSS 7638/13, BD to RS, 25 November 1984). The last sentence is the perfect summation of Davis's attitude to authors; it is likely she would have been uncomfortable with the kind of attention that both Kent's biography and this Element shine on her work, as I have already mentioned.

One of the few reviews of Park's work that directly engages with the writing and its themes, as opposed to her personal life,[10] appeared in the *Australian Book Review* in 2009 on the re-release of the *Harp in the South* trilogy. The review is largely complimentary of Park's work but does take issue with some of the writing in *Missus*, using the word 'melodramatic' twice in the space of as many paragraphs (Walker, 2009: 26). This review shares some of the same concerns that Davis raised in her edit and that Park rejected. The exchange indicates that particularly later in an author's career, they are in a position to reject edits and so the judgement of a work rests more squarely with them since it is often a less collaborative process than for a younger writer. Unlike *Swords*, there is no extant correspondence that stipulates publication was contingent on editorial changes.

While authors might be less likely to accept edits at the later stages of their careers, in the case of *Missus*, Park's dismissal of edits seems less to do with a sensitivity to prose being perfect and not in need of editing and more to do with a sense that the editor and the author were not simpatico when it came to envisioning the style and aims of the book. This connects to McCormack's (2006: 53) focus on 'sensibility' or how an editor 'tastes and judges'.

---

[10] A description of Park as 'handsome, happily married to a famous writer, a capable housewife, the mother of five children and a highly successful writer herself' is indicative of the general tenor of commentary in contemporary reviews.' (Bulletin 1961, np)

Conclusion

The interactions between Park and Davis illustrate the ambivalent nature of editorial dynamics by demonstrating the kinds of negotiations and hierarchies of priorities at play in the publishing process, for the author, the editor and the publisher alike. Paying attention to the Davis edits shows that the draft Park delivered to Thomas Nelson was significantly longer, had a key Protestant character and was the result of careful and sustained research. Park agreed to most of Davis's edits relating to Mr Moy but rejected those that would have lessened the focus on Jackie's short stature or descriptions of the Depression and the suffering that poor people of the time endured.

The relationship between Park and Davis spanned friendship and a professional collaboration: it was both personal and aesthetic. Although Park could have insisted on her version without explanation, she was always careful to offer reasoned explanations for her rejections of edits, namely her planning and care in drafting, her experience as a bookseller and her vision for the book as a whole. She was savvy in her responses, spotting the arbitrariness of cuts of a given number of words, and she resisted changes that were not in keeping with her vision for the book – a book that ultimately went on to sell well in Australia, find publishers overseas and recognition with awards.

2 Revisioning History: The Editor as Social Barometer in Thea Astley's *The Multiple Effects of Rainshadow*

Introduction

Although books on editing cover a range of roles that editors inhabit over the life of a book, such as mentor, friend, bank and psychologist (c.f. Munro, 2021; Athill, 2011; Gottlieb, 2016), as well as a number of intellectual and emotional tools they use, such as sensibility or instinct (c.f. McCormack, 2006; Brett, 2011), one of the aspects of the practice that does not receive much attention is the editor as social barometer. Along with all the other roles and modes, editors are responsible for considering how literary and commercial markets will respond to the author's engagement with politically fraught subject matter, the position of characters from marginalised backgrounds, and the language the author uses to produce the work. They are anticipating the Bourdiesian field (Bourdieu and Johnson, 1993: 49) in all of the processes of editing and, in some cases, undertaking work with a view to managing the work's position in the field. Naturally, their habitus has a significant role in determining their own engagement with a given text. In the Australian context, these questions are most fraught when it comes to non-Indigenous or settler authors representing Indigenous characters and events of violence, dispossession and other mistreatment.

Thea Astley is often used as an example of an author whose work becomes more progressive over the course of their lifetime (Dale, 2008: 150; Sheridan, 2011: 19; Lever, 2008: 144). This is especially so in the final two books of her career, which were released after the Mabo decision of 3 June 1992 that replaced *terra nullius* with pre-existing native title as an Australian legal principle; Paul Keating's plea for racial justice in his Redfern speech of 10 December 1992; the United Nations' Proclamation of 1993 as the 'Year of Indigenous Peoples'; and the opening in 1995 of the inquiry that led two years later to the tabling of the *Bringing Them Home Report* (Taylor, 2021: 3). Critic Cheryl Taylor's summary of key moments in settler–Indigenous relations in the 1990s, from which I drew the preceding list, emphasises just how many key changes took place in a few short years. This was all just after the 1988 bicentenary of Captain Cook's arrival in Australia, and at a time when significant attention was given to the settler–Indigenous dynamic in Australian society.

Astley's career is recognisable as a model that contemporary creative writers follow. After completing an Arts degree and working as a teacher she wrote novels and taught creative writing at Macquarie University in Sydney for many years (Lamb, 2015). From her oft-republished lecture 'Being a Queenslander' (1978) through her choice of the north-eastern state as the setting for her books, Astley fits into a tradition alongside David Malouf, Jessica Anderson and Janette Turner Hospital. For her use of rich and textured prose, Astley can be compared with Patrick White or Randolph Stow (Perkins, 1992: 14). She has won the equal highest number of Miles Franklin Awards – four, matching Tim Winton – and she remains a fixture on reading lists at schools and universities. Aside from writing about non-Indigenous and Indigenous relations, she was also concerned with feminism in *An Item from the Late News* (1982); the role of the artist in *The Acolyte* (1972) and intergenerational legacies in *It's Raining in Mango* (1987). Her writing is often polyphonic, although it usually centres male characters since, as she explained in one interview, she wanted to write books that men would not be embarrassed to read on a plane (Gilbert, 1988: 110).

Astley's novel *The Multiple Effects of Rainshadow* was acquired by Bob Sessions at Penguin (formerly of Thomas Nelson) and, according to Astley's biographer, Karen Lamb (2015: 296), it was edited 'at Penguin' before the copyedit was undertaken by Meredith Rose. While the proof-read pages are held at the Fryer Library, University of Queensland, along with other material, I do not have the name of the proofreader. From the records at the Fryer, it would appear that the work had a fairly standard path from structural editing through copyediting and then proofreading.

Astley's penultimate novel, *The Multiple Effects of Rainshadow* (1996) won *The Age* book of the year and has been reissued in the Text Classics series, which is the edition quoted from in this section (Astley, 2018a). Set on Doebin, a renamed Palm Island, this novel is a polyphonic work, collecting stories from an ensemble cast, all of whom came to live on the island over the span of a few decades starting in the 1930s. The opening section, and passages between each chapter, consists of an italicised interjection written in non-standard English from the perspective of Manny Cooktown, an Indigenous man with a key role in the narrative: he had protected his fellow Indigenous and non-Indigenous islanders by killing the official, Superintendent Brodie, who had murdered his family and then rampaged across the island. The story is closely based on the real-life tale of Peter Prior, told by his daughter in *Straight from the Yudaman's Mouth* (1993), and Astley lists the book in her acknowledgments. The novel's narrative also includes Mrs Curthoys, who runs a boarding house, her two daughters, the Catholic priest Father Donnellan and a schoolteacher named Vine. Later the work includes sections from the next generation including Normie Cooktown, Manny's son.

The chapters come from different perspectives; most of the characters are reflecting on the main incident and related events many years after they take place. The work opens with close third-person narration from Manny Cooktown, an Indigenous resident of the island. Sections from his perspective punctuate the text, appearing between each chapter from the perspective of settler-colonial characters. The novel ends with a song that Manny's son Normie has created, using local Language.[11] The refrain is: 'We do not understand' (2018a: 281) because Indigenous residents of the island have been taken there from across Queensland and could not communicate in Language with each other.

Perhaps the most significant of the editorial interventions in *Multiple Effects* relates to the Aboriginal characters in the book, and to Manny Cooktown and his descendants in particular. There has been criticism that both praises and takes issue with Astley's approach to these characters and it is unlikely that a book written in this way would be published in the current climate, although not impossible of course. Rose's suggestion to change the Manny sections from first- to third-person mark a significant difference between versions and, coupled with the shift from 'native' to 'black' and 'Murri' to 'black' seem to paint a picture of the editor as intermediary between the author's vision and the demands of the marketplace of ideas at a given time and social context.

---

[11] In Australia, 'Language' refers to Indigenous languages.

Although there is a general expectation that an editor will draw in an author who has gone too far in their use of metaphors or elaborate imagery, in the case of Thea Astley, the archive shows that even in the books with her most extravagant prose, Astley's editors did little to change her style. We can see that there are even instances where Astley added more descriptive language at the copyedit stage.

A New Ally: Editing as Collaboration

Unlike other writers of her generation, it seems that Astley predominantly worked with female editors. The many different editors who contributed to her work include Beatrice Davis at Angus & Robertson and Thomas Nelson, Jackie Yowell at University of Queensland Press and Meredith Rose at Penguin/Viking. She did collaborate with male publishers, such as Laurie Hergenhan at University of Queensland Press and Bob Sessions at Angus & Robertson, and Karen Lamb (2015: 214) recounts Astley's run-in with Richard Walsh when he helmed A&R, but overwhelmingly her experience of being edited was with other women.

From the edits carried out by Beatrice Davis for *A Descant for Gossips*, *The Well Dressed Explorer*, *The Slow Natives*, *A Boatload of Home Folk* and *Hunting the Wild Pineapple*, most of the work could be described as copy-editing (UQFL 97/1–26). Astley's archive does not reveal requests for significant changes to characterisation, plot or style; most of the edits are either correcting typos or suggesting a replacement word. Perhaps the most significant of Davis's edits across these titles is in suggesting a new title for one of Astley's short stories, which went on to form the title of her collection *Hunting the Wild Pineapple* (UQFL 97/3/25: 50).

For *The Multiple Effects of Rainshadow* she returned to Penguin, having been signed by Bob Sessions (the same person Beatrice Davis corresponded with about Ruth Park and the Literature Board). He had been publisher at Nelson when Astley's *A Kindness Cup* (1974) was published. Astley had been signed both by major trade houses such as Penguin and by independent presses such as University of Queensland Press. While she spoke highly of Beatrice Davis (MLMSS 2808, 1974) her esteem for an editor was only one of the reasons for choosing a publisher; the size of the advance and the systems in place to promote her work were also relevant factors. By the time she was published by Penguin in the 1990s, her advances were quite significant: $30,000 each for *Multiple Effects* and *Drylands* (UQFL 46/297).

It was at Penguin that Astley discovered 'a new ally' as Karen Lamb (2015: 296) puts it. At the time, Meredith Rose was a relatively young editor but she and Astley 'clicked'. The significance of this relationship is borne out by the acknowledgement in *Multiple Effects* (Astley, 2018a: 2), which is the only time that Astley ever thanks an editor, and by the fact that Rose was asked to edit Astley's last book, *Drylands*, even though she had moved to the other side of the country by then to work for another publishing house (Lamb, 2015: 302).

Editing as an Impulse to Simplify

For much of her career, criticism of Astley's work focused on the question of her purple prose – the use of metaphors that some deemed extravagant or unnecessary. One example of this negative response is the case of fellow author Helen Garner (1982: 22), who found herself driven 'berserk' by Astley's novel, *An Item from the Late News*. But my examination of Astley's archive shows that in many of her books, her editors left metaphors, similes and other such authorial devices largely untouched.

While it's impossible to know whether critics would have taken issue with Astley's style and the richness of her writing if she had been male, oftentimes critics seem to dislike the prose not because it fails the author's ambitions or because it is poorly executed but because it is not in line with their personal taste. Critic J. M. Couper (2008: 37) thought that 'words like *ovately*, are too often like ocean liners sitting in shallow waters: their circumstances do not support them'. He did not just take issue with Astley's word choice; he was also saying that she was 'straining after terms and metaphors that are picked up like pretty shells, but that do not serve what she has to say' (38). He was not alone in taking issue with Astley's unusual or sophisticated vocabulary; reviewers David Conley (1986: n.p.) and Diana McRobbie (1983: n.p.) would have preferred less unusual vocabulary and simpler expression. While it can be argued that

Astley uses words for their own sake rather than to directly further the characterisation and plot, it is also clear that Astley, like authors she stated she admired such as Nabokov or Flaubert (Miner 1988: n.p.), played with words for the sake of the language game itself; for her own pleasure and the pleasure of like-minded readers. Would critics have taken exception to Astley's word choice if her books had been set in Paris or London instead of small-town Queensland? My sense is that there is an expectation for a certain kind of storytelling connected to place and that such language and sensibility is not seen as native to Queensland.

For the most part, her editors left such embellishment untouched: however, in the case of *Beachmasters* (1985) the editor noted that Astley had used sixteen foreign words on pages three, four and five, and suggested that the resultant feeling of unfamiliarity would be too much for readers, suggesting that she should change a few instances in the interests of accessibility (UQFL 97/5). Astley did not reduce the number of foreign words in the book's opening pages. Meredith Rose was fairly restrained in her suggestions about trimming or removing descriptions or poetic language, but there are instances where she suggested deletions and Astley followed her advice, as I will detail later in this chapter.

There is also a question about the ambition of the work. Astley's ambition always seems to have been high literature, with its focus on form and style, language play and formal experimentation. This is carried through until the end of her career when *Drylands* (1999) included postmodern tenets of play, meta-fiction and intertextuality. *Multiple Effects* was Astley's last book before *Drylands*, and also engages in formal experimentation in its juxtaposition of different voices, its play with time and perspective and its post-colonial interrogations of relationships to place, environment and people. The edits operate in a way sympathetic to that aim, not interrupting rich language and description nor touching the structure.[12]

---

[12] In Karen Lamb's (2015) biography of Astley, she notes that the manuscript had 'already been worked on in the process of being bought by Penguin' (296). I have not examined this text because of travel restrictions during the period of writing, due to the COVID-19 pandemic. I would be surprised if these were dramatic

Given the tendency towards such language in Astley's earlier works, and the fact that authors are often edited less in later works, one might expect that Astley's later books would have more of her literary flourishes than novels such as *Girl with a Monkey* or *The Well Dressed Explorer*. However, *Multiple Effects* does not demonstrate this, either in the finished version, which Debra Adelaide (1996: 10s) praised as 'accessible', or in the edited typescript. There are relatively few instances of Rose removing language that might be considered particularly descriptive or rich.

Three examples of such editing come in the first half of the book. The first is when Rose suggested changing the phrase 'describing a parabola of invitation' to 'gestures' (UQFL 97/17/105: 10). The change is not simply about reducing a phrase of five words to a single verb, but also changes a visual description deploying maths and a sort of courtly formality into plain English. Another example is when Rose suggests removing the simile 'stabs of delicious pain like a rocket in screaming stars of red and orange' (110). Arguably this is a mixed metaphor, first describing the pain as a rocket and then saying that the rocket is made out of stars. Also, from a plausibility perspective, we know that stars do not scream, given the vacuum of space. Rose transplants the word 'delicious' from describing pain to describing the stabs, keeping a sense of the perverse pleasure in pain but simplifying the sentence significantly (116).

The last example is a suggested trim to reduce the wordiness of a sentence and to remove the repetition of one word. The edits are marked with strikethrough and the insertions are italicised.

> 'In one of those pauses between cloud-bursts, ~~clouds~~ *nimbus* peeled back like stage drapes and a watery moon ~~lighting the garden subjected us to~~ *lit* drama too melodramatic to be believ~~able~~*ed*.' *(46)*

Again, this is an instance of replacing six words with one to make a sentence more straightforward. That said, Rose did not touch the mixed

changes given her past record of edits and the continuity between the drafts and the edited typescript in the Fryer holding.

metaphor of a 'watery moon' and 'stage drape' clouds. While editors may be taught that mixed metaphors should be avoided, in the case of a writer like Astley the prose is generally quite dense with description and it is this kind of evocative image that surely contributed to the overall impression that led eminent Australian literature scholar Elizabeth Webby to describe *Multiple Effects* as 'poetical and musical' (quoted in Lamb, 2015: 299).

Overwhelmingly, Rose's edits were minor nicks and cuts rather than slashes or major extractions. She cut descriptions such as 'a Conrad character, foul-mouthed, foul-breathed' (UQFL 97/17/105: 209) and 'His eyes charted her coast but wanted to try the inland of her. All that within seconds. He had to look away from eating up surfaces' (186). Over the course of the work, there are relatively few instances of these cuts and Astley's rich, detailed prose with word play, Latinate vocabulary and linguistic jokes remain.

One of the interesting findings from the archive is that Astley was not always moving towards greater simplicity. In the draft for *Multiple Effects* she raised the register of the prose on a few occasions such as when 'ploughed' became 'furrowed', 'Down under' became 'in the Antipodes' And 'Mate' became 'friend' (UQFL 97/16: 61). This proves that the editing and revising process is not unidirectional, that in the iterative stages, there can be shifts both to great simplicity and to more poetic language.

While it is the case that editors often make suggestions that authors ignore or dismiss, in Astley's case, her archive shows that, for the most part, her editors were sympathetic with her style and did not frequently suggest changes to her prose, even where such changes would have appeased some of the critics of Astley's work. This differs significantly from what we will see in the next chapter, where Jessica Anderson's editor suggests change to style and voice, and she reacted very strongly against their requests.

Murri to Black

Significantly, one of the changes on the typescript related to Indigenous characters and their representation is that in Astley's draft there were repeated references to 'Murris' and 'natives' but in the marked-up copyedit, the word was changed to 'black'. 'Murri' is an Aboriginal English word for an Indigenous person from the north-eastern part of the continent (Dixon, Ramson, Thomas, 1992: 172). Over the course of the book there are at least fifteen of these changes. On two occasions there is a change from 'Murri' to 'abos' (UQFL 97/17/105: 110, 115).

Without correspondence in the archive outlining the reasons for such changes, and given that the editor has not been able to recall details about the editorial process,[13] I cannot say precisely why such changes were made, but I can make informed suppositions. There are a few potential reasons for this shift. One is a concern that the book's readership would be unfamiliar with the term. However, a Google Ngram of the word 'Murri' shows that there have been a few spikes in usage over the more than 200 years of colonisation (see Appendix). The largest spike by far is around the 1890s, but there have been smaller spikes around the bicentenary and around the year 2000. Although a rather blunt measure, the Ngram suggests that there was a fair amount of usage of the word at the time that *Multiple Effects* was being edited. Another potential reason is that, in anticipation of the book's publication in the US (as many of Astley's books had been by the time *Multiple Effects* was in production), perhaps the word was changed since 'black' would not need to be amended or glossed for a foreign audience.

A closer look at some specific examples of the edits demonstrates just how the change impacts on the text. In the published version of the book, in a section narrated in close third person from the perspective of Morrow, a radio broadcaster, we read, 'The rollcalling of his gangs of resentful black workers . . . (Astley, 2018: 73).' In the typescript, the parenthetical aside '(it took time for him to learn to call them Murris)' (UQFL 97/17/105: 72) follows on. Removing this reference is consistent with the general change to remove the word from the book but it also removes a degree of nuance about the character learning Language, as well as a representation of the shift in power dynamics that comes with a settler character addressing Indigenous characters by the word they use to describe themselves. The idea that Morrow would use 'Murri', that it took time for him to acclimatise to the word, puts him in a more sympathetic light, despite other short-comings to which the reader may respond. It is worth considering this as

---

[13] Meredith Rose, email to the author, 6 July 2021.

a factor in relation to the change of the word 'native', which was also switched to black on more than a dozen occasions throughout the novel. While the real-world people on whom the characters in Astley's novel were based may well have used that word to describe Indigenous people, the decision to change it, despite the fact that *Multiple Effects* is a work of historical fiction, is consistent with a general move to create a text that is more politically correct.

The two changes, considered in tandem, raise the question: was the change from 'Murri' to 'black' a manoeuvre to avoid a sense of cultural appropriation? 'Native' is clearly pejorative and, even though *Multiple Effects* is a work of historical fiction, perhaps the repetition of this word had a cumulative effect on Rose as the book's embodied reader. It is plausible, and consistent, that the change from 'Murri' was to avoid a sense of appropriation.

First to Third Person

Perhaps the most significant change that editor Meredith Rose suggested for the manuscript of *Multiple Effects* was the shift from collective first to third person in the sections narrated from Manny Cooktown's perspective. There is no correspondence in the archive that explains the suggested change but there is also no sign that Astley took issue with it. Indeed, since Rose is the only publishing professional that Astley thanks in the acknowledgements, one might conclude that Astley was pleased with Rose's work.

I have not found any criticism that references the fact that Manny's sections, while written from his point of view, are not in first person. Indeed, critic Geoff Rodoreda (2018: 135) remarks that Manny's segments 'are "spoken"' as if Manny is directly addressing the reader. Careful attention to the prose reveals that this is not the case. While these sections are mostly in non-standard English and they are italicised, almost as if the reader is eavesdropping on Manny's thoughts, they are not presented as speech and they are not narrated in the same way as other sections of the book. In her contemporaneous book review, Debra Adelaide mentioned Manny's sections as 'another narrative thread, which gives brief glimpses in the yearning puzzled heart of Manny Cooktown' (1996: 10s). The distance of third person does not stop Adelaide from seeing, albeit briefly, into the character's heart.

The book opens with direct speech (although not in quote marks): 'The blue fire, he said. This blue. Burn my heart it jump like fish jumping straight down.' A few sentences later come Rose's first change of perspective, as marked on the copyedited typescript: 'In the mornin after ~~we~~ *they* creep out from behind the rocks where ~~we~~ *they* shelter all night, the bodies' (UQFL 97/17/105: 1). The rest of the section was written in collective first person and changed to collective third person, except for one instance where Manny says: 'All night too they rattle and the smells get bad in the little place ~~we~~ *they* sit and ~~I~~ *he* wet ~~myself~~ *himself* just thinkin' (2). Here we shift from first-person singular to third-person singular. With collective first person there is already a degree of indeterminacy, an imprecision about who is speaking. Changing it to collective third person creates further distance between the narrator and the subject. This could represent either an increase in the power differential, or the insertion of space between character and author, in order to ease any possible perceptions of cultural appropriation.

Later in the work, more instances of first person and collective first also change to third and collective third respectively. This section concludes:

> ~~But~~ *He* forget that year but the next he take us them and when ~~we~~ *they* got pay too, more than when ~~we~~ *they* see ~~our~~ *their* wives an kids everythin all right.
>
> ~~We~~ *They* got pay too, more than ~~we~~ *they* ever got on Doebin workin for the gubbamin. That make Jeannie happy. Then ~~I~~ *he* remember mumma say, Happy don't last. *(194)*

There is clearly a greater distance between 'we' and 'they', regardless of whether the text is rendered in non-standard or standard English – for example, the shift in the final line of this section from a character remembering what his own mother said – and the distance registers with the reader, even if only on an unconscious level. However the choice of Aboriginal English coming from the perspective of an Aboriginal character evokes a kind of immediacy to the text, and it could be argued that the shift to third person affords a little more room to potentially counter accusations of cultural appropriation.

The choice still prompted discussion. In analysis of *Rainshadow*, Sheridan (2016) comments:

> Although the Indigenous men in Astley's novel can speak . . .
> their access to the symbolic order is different from that of the
> (relatively) powerless white women. This difference between
> the white woman and the black man's access to the power of
> discourse is dramatised in *Rainshadow*: even though Normie
> has an education and is not afraid of the whites, he does not
> speak in the same register of power as them. *(144)*

While Mrs Curthoys, as manager of the boarding house, is socially below Brodie, Vine and Donnellan, in the section that she narrates in first person she is keen to point out that her speech and comportment surprise her peers; in one instance she says of the doctor, 'I think my vowels have confounded him, brought him to social heel, as it were' (UQFL 97/17/105: 20). We may gather from that detail that if there is a distinction between different kinds of settler English, any non-standard English would attract even greater disdain and lead to greater disempowerment.

In brief, the Indigenous characters in the book do not have power in the same way as the non-Indigenous characters and do not have the control of a first-person narration of their own story. Although the Indigenous men can and do speak, in the sense that there is direct dialogue in the Manny sections and elsewhere in the book, the Aboriginal men never narrate their own story directly to the reader as the white characters do. Manny was given this voice in the book's draft but in the version that went to print, his personal pronoun almost never appears. This adds to the discrepancy of power between the white characters – even the women – and the black characters. Even though Leonie and Mrs Curthoys are generally operating at the mercy of the men in their lives, they have the agency of telling their stories directly to the reader. It is not the case for Manny. While the 'I' may be implied in his sections, it never actually appears and so he does not have 'voice' or control over his own story in the way that the other characters do.

Rose's edits keep Astley's version of non-standard English, even while shifting perspective. One example occurs with the edit: 'Thirty now. Father Donnellan tell ~~me~~ *him* thirty . . . Them people Italian. Look bit like ~~us~~ *them*, *like Willie, like Hector.* But the day she smile, eh, and show ~~us our~~ *them* rooms in shed' (UQFL 97/17/17: 193). Further, Rose added a degree of distance by choosing Willie and Hector as the examples and not naming Manny. This fits with Manny being a kind of unnamed, unvoiced narrator of the section.

In many cases, Rose removed the pronoun so that the speaker is implied rather than clearly stated. There is not ownership over the words, as in the case of the author or the character articulating their pronoun. Chloe Hooper, in her introduction to the recent Text Classics edition of *Multiple Effects*, speculates: 'The sections written in Aboriginal English will strike some contemporary readers as evocative but others will regard the style as unfortunate cultural appropriation' (Astley, 2018a: xii). If there is a concern about ventriloquising an Aboriginal character or speaking on behalf of Aboriginal people, then perhaps by removing the pronoun, Rose's shift to greater indeterminacy was not just about widening the narrative voice to potentially belonging to more people but avoiding perceived cultural appropriation. In this way, the editor would be the intermediary between the expectations of readers, reviewers and scholars and the author's original text.

Since the book was published in the 1990s and discussions of the responsibilities of settler writers to Aboriginal subjects were well under way (take, for instance, Modjeska's and Williams' critiques of *Coonardoo* as Jeanine Leane (2014: 5) has described) Rose was likely acting in the interests of amending the work to make it more appropriate to the cultural market of the day. Although the editor does not have a detailed recollection of the reason for the change or whether it was her or the author who was the instigator (Meredith Rose, personal communication, 6 July 2021), the change at the copyedit stage can be read as a shift to increase the distance between author and subject.

The Historical Traces

A relevant question for Astley's engagement with Indigenous culture concerns the sources she used to create the work and the way she interpreted them in her fiction. As mentioned earlier, *Multiple Effects* is the only book in which Astley credits her editor, though it is not the only book in which she acknowledges the historical texts that have been a basis for her creative work. It is not generally within the copyeditor's remit to check the source materials so it is unlikely that Rose would have read the books that Astley cites in her acknowledgements. If anything, it probably would have been reassuring to see the kinds of works that Astley cited there.

The publishing history and paratexts associated with *Multiple Effects* reveal important details about the book itself, its publishing process and the industry more broadly. For this material, using the approach of genetic criticism affords useful insights. Over the course of her career Astley wrote three novels that were sparked by historical events and the differences and similarities between these books reveal important changes in the impact of defamation law, the shifts in cultural conversation and Astley's own treatment of historical material. Thanks to the archive at the Fryer Library to which Astley submitted material over a period of decades, we can observe some of her processes as well as extrapolate from that to consider the effects of laws and social trends more broadly.

By the time she was drafting *Multiple Effects*, Astley had already been leaving her draft materials at the Fryer for a number of years. *Multiple Effects* is the third of her novels inspired by historical events (the other two being *The Kindness Cup* and *Beachmasters*) and Astley not only kept articles but also annotated notes for the benefit of presenting the archive to future researchers.

As well as keeping material relating to her research, Astley annotated some of it for the archive. For instance, she included a typed page 'From My Life and Times. Octave Six 1923–1930 by Compton McKenzie' (UQFL97/17)'. Astley handwrites on the same page: 'This extract was seminal for the section on the publisher in M.E. of Rainshadow.' She continues by commenting that the librarian at Nowra Library also helped source *My Island of Dreams* by J. W. Fringo 'who apparently settled later on the same island (as far as I could ascertain!) during the period Robert Currie was still alive and working as superintendent on Palm. Fingo, plus wife & daughter, lasted only a few months & returned to T'Ville.' On the reverse of the page, Astley added, 'I'm not sure of the sequence in which

Greening and Bring were in the Palm Group. However, there had an author (crummy!) and a publisher. Ergo ... How could I resist?' Here Astley is commenting on her drawing out a potential story from the facts that she could trace and her decision to include a note in the archive reflects a desire to generate a kind of map for the project of her novel and its relationship with the historical record. As Cheryl Taylor (2021: 12) noted, Astley quoted settler sources verbatim, which is very different from her choice to recast Indigenous tellings of the events of Palm Island in non-standard English.

In *Straight from the Yudaman's Mouth*, there is a description of Peter Prior confronting a well-armed John Curry, the superintendent who was armed and killing people on the island: 'I don't know how I managed to say it, but I said to him "Hey Boss, surrender"' (Prior, 1993: 21). In *Multiple Effects*, the same exchange is rendered:

> 'Manny remember the word he was supposed to say.
> 'He call, Surrender. He call, Put down your gun.'
> *(UQFL 97/17/105: 130)*

Clearly the Prior account of the event puts the Indigenous man in a position of control, both of the English language and of his own actions. The Astley version shifts agency by saying that Manny says what he was 'supposed to say' and makes Manny simply a conduit for settler intentions. In the same scene, Curry says to Prior, 'Peter, you are lucky to got [sic] me first, you black bastard, before I got you. But why did they use you to do their dirty work?' (Prior, 1993: 21). When Astley writes the exchange Manny says 'And Uncle Boss he say, "That all right, Manny. Those bastards made you do it"' (UQFL 97/17/105: 131). While the word 'bastards' appears in each utterance, Curry uses it to describe Prior, whereas in the Astley version Brodie uses it to describe the other non-Indigenous men on Palm Island. Again, there is a shift in agency here, albeit a smaller change than in the previously cited quote.

Since Astley left the archive with her research and cited these books in her Acknowledgements, she was leaving a trail of breadcrumbs for researchers to follow, as Susan Sheridan and Cheryl Taylor have indeed done. The difficulty is that the settler critics who have responded seem to have assumed that Astley was reintroducing Prior's account into the language he used. However, in a 1997 documentary, which shares its name with the book that tells his story, Prior speaks in the standard English of the book. He does not sound like Manny Cooktown. Astley has made a choice to change the language that Renarta Prior uses to align with her idea of how an Indigenous man in that setting would have spoken.

It is also noteworthy that these scholars, while interested in changes to the work through drafting (Taylor, 2009: 56), did not consider the kinds of changes that were part of the editorial process, as if only the amendments that can be traced to the author are important when analysing the work. Taylor (2021: 7) comments dismissively about the edits saying that 'Astley and her Viking editor Rose continued to make small changes to Manny's language into the novel's copy-editing stages'. My argument is that these changes are not small and that they deserve attention for the information they impart about editing, about Indigenous and non-Indigenous relations in Australia and the process of producing creative work. These edits, and the way they shed light on the social and creative climate in which the work was produced, demonstrate the importance of combining the methodology of genetic criticism with an examination of professional editing.

Although it would not have been the responsibility of the editor to check that the sources were used in a sensitive fashion, it is useful to see the ways in which there are tensions between attempts to make work that is culturally sensitive and work that includes Indigenous characters, and real Indigenous experience, as part of the storytelling. This study is also representative of the benefits of genetic criticism in literary studies in that it can confirm or subvert orthodoxy in scholarly responses to a given text. The finding vindicates the work of genetic criticism both in terms of what it explains about the literary work and the author's process more broadly.

Conclusion

Paying attention to the archival record affords an insight into the kinds of suggestions that editors make in their role as social barometer. This is particularly notable with an author who was published over five decades, as Thea Astley was. Taking Astley's paratexts into consideration also creates a clearer understanding of the decisions that the author made as she was constructing her characters out of historical records, both Indigenous and non-Indigenous. Just as Park's editors were concerned that readers may not engage with a protagonist who is different from them, Thea Astley's editor and publisher would have been conscious of the discussions around Indigenous representation and cultural appropriation that were a loud national conversation in the Australia of the 1990s. As I have previously stated, the maxim in professional editing holds that the work is always ultimately the responsibility of the author. While it is true, the editor, with their personal experience and their responsibility to the publisher that pays their wage, has an important role in working to align a given text with the social norms of the day in the interests of the work, its reception and the author's reputation.

3 Openings and Closing: Editing as Expansive and Limiting in the Editing of *Tirra Lirra by the River*

It is a pity that the amateurish beginning wasn't edited to the standard of the rest – it would have been a much better book.

(Bedford, 1978: 41)

Introduction

Rather than looking only to outlier cases in the study of editing, such as Maxwell Perkins and Thomas Wolfe or Gordon Lish and Raymond Carver, it is important for students of editing and scholars alike to examine the contributions of editors operating within the standard range of intervention that most contemporary books receive. This case study demonstrates the ways that editorial intervention, at the structural and line-editing levels, can open possibilities for a text, and close them, across the span of the editorial process. It illustrates that editorial work can range from the prompt of a single sentence to the potential introduction of errors and mischaracterisations in a text and emphasises that editorial work is often undertaken by multiple individuals over the course of a book's production; embodied agents who oftentimes have different sensibilities and ideas about the style, expression and mode of a text.

In this chapter the subject is *Tirra Lirra by the River*, an award-winning novel by Jessica Anderson that has been praised by scholars, set on school and university courses and been in print since it was first published in 1978. By tracing the evolution of the work through the archive, we can see how one comment from someone who was not even professionally engaged as the book's editor led to its most significant change. We can also see that the person paid to copyedit the book made suggestions for changes that ran contrary to the author's intention and were ultimately countermanded. *Tirra Lirra* is not an exceptional case, and it is precisely because the editorial contribution – which alternatively opened possibilities or overdetermined the text – demonstrates the potential power of suggestions by working editors and the potential harm that can arise from a misunderstanding of the author's project. It demonstrates to scholars the contribution of actors other than the author themselves, even in the case of a relatively minor comment, and confirms some of the assertions that textual editors make about the corruption of texts at the hands of editors and others in the production process.

There are three editors who worked on *Tirra Lirra*, according to my findings. Alan Maclean was not employed to edit the book but gave feedback that led to significant changes to the work. Susan Nicholls corresponded with Jessica Anderson about the work, operating in the role of 'project editor'; namely, someone who manages the manuscript on its path to publication, but who does not necessarily edit it themselves. The copyeditor was Pamela Reid. As with Ruth Park's *Swords and Crowns and Rings*, it is likely there was a proofreader but the proofread pages are not held with the rest of the archive.

Greenberg (2018: 21) emphasises that an editor is an embodied agent who has a part in representing the publisher, the text and sometimes the author, depending on the context. One of the important findings of this chapter is the potential conflict between embodied agents working on the book, their readings of the work, and the resulting potential clash of sensibilities. Since the standard practice in trade publishing is to have different editors involved at different stages of the process (structural, copy, proofreaders), there will be different perspectives from each of these agents who exert influence on the work. This chapter shows that editing work is highly contingent and the potential development or hindrance of a text from editorial intervention depends on the editors themselves and the author's response to their comments.

Anderson's Editors

It is unusual for a writer to change style with nearly every book they publish, and surely a difficulty for the publisher. With literary fiction titles the publisher has only the author as a marketing tool and a description of the story itself, so without the ballast of the editor's reputation these books are a difficult sell.

This is not to say that Anderson discounted the potential role of an editor. In an interview, she responded to the question 'Do you think editors are important in fiction?' with the following comments:

Yes, I do. I think they're most important. I don't like the
kind of editors that are reputed to exist in America, who
will take a book and alter it completely for the market. But
often I could have done in my life with a person to whom
I could show something when I was in trouble, and even if
they didn't suggest the right thing, to talk about it is often
a – to talk with a knowledgeable and sympathetic person.
I think if a writer has an editor of that kind it's a great help,
but of course they're almost as rare as good writers.

(Ellison, 1986: 42–3)

When Anderson refers to the American style, she may well have been
talking about the Maxwell Perkins/Thomas Wolfe model. The degree of
Gordon Lish's intervention in Raymond Carver's work was not widely
known at the time Anderson gave the interview; perhaps she had spoken
with American peers about their experiences. Notably, unlike American
authors whose editorial experience has been the subject of study, Anderson
did not benefit from the advocacy of a champion who could represent her
work over a number of years because she changed publishers – in this case,
switching from Macmillan UK to Macmillan Australia, and later to
Penguin.[14] As a result of shifting publishers, Anderson did not have an
editor to whom she always turned for advice and feedback over the course
of her career. In the same interview she says she did not have any
particularly close writer friends and so we are left to conclude that throughout her writing life, the drafting process was predominantly solitary for her.
From these comments, you may imagine that editing had little impact on
Anderson's experience of publishing but a study of the archive as presented
here reveals that is only part of the story.

Since editorial intervention was not the driving force in her drafting
process, the impetus must have come from within. When asked about her
habits, Anderson replied, 'I do very little correcting on the proofs.

---

[14] Another of her books would have been published by Bodley Head in the UK if
Collins in Australia had agreed to take it on, but Collins did not accept and so the
manuscript was never published (Ellison, 1986: 31).

But I make changes on all the drafts, not single words so much as whole pages. If I'm desperate, and I often am, I'll do a lot of retyping or rewriting, to get that kind of impetus, hoping that at some point it will just come right' (Grenville and Wolfe, 2001: 12). This is borne out by the archive since both notebooks at the National Library and at the Mitchell Library (the two main holdings of Anderson's papers) include pages where Anderson has written and rewritten the same section with only minor changes between the different versions.

Anderson's first book was published by Alan Maclean at Macmillan UK, and the two that followed were published by Lord Hardinge of Penshurst (who always referred to himself as such in their correspondence). Maclean had suggested Anderson send her manuscript to his colleague George Hardinge, since he knew he was setting up a crime list at Macmillan (MLMSS 3773 Add on 2040, 4 September 1969). The archives show that Hardinge and Anderson had an occasionally testy relationship and a few exchanges over royalty arrangements, paperback publishing as well as a string of letters about the disappointing performance of *The Last Man's Head* and even worse sales for *The Commandant*. A further point of contention was that *The Commandant* had a thoroughly inappropriate cover and a printing error so significant that an erratum slip had to be included with the book as it was processed through the warehouse on its way to bookstores (MLMSS 3773 Add on 2040, 23 April 1975).

In terms of editorial intervention, there are only two notes on the file where Hardinge has made suggestions of an editorial nature. He suggested a change to the title of *The Last Man's Head* (initially entitled *The Winner*, MLMSS 3773 Add on 2040, 3 October 1969), and the second note included a few suggestions about *The Commandant*. Crucially, his editorial suggestions can be read as a clashing of male and female sensibilities for he writes, 'Towards the end I think it is a bit anti-climactic in that really the male parts are best but we are stuck at some length with the women and children' (MLMSS 3773 Add on 2040, undated). It would appear to be an instance where the author and editor have different opinions about the nature of the book.

Hardinge's approach contravenes both textual editors' edicts and the commonly described edicts of professional editing as well. Certainly,

Hardinge is not working with the author's 'final intentions' as his guiding principle but nor is he working for a best version of the work, in accordance with Mandy Brett's expression of the process as quoted at the start of this Element. Hardinge is imagining a particular kind of reader, one who is disinterested in the female characters and the children with whom they spend time. His version of the reader is at odds with the reader who Anderson has conjured with her draft.

Further, the archive shows that Anderson did not enjoy structural editing support either from her publishers or from her agents. Anderson engaged Campbell Thomson and McLaughlin for representation for *The Commandant* but although there are friendly letters between Anderson and Stephanie Townsend, a literary agent, there is no record of suggestions relating to drafting, intervention with the publishers to manage the misprint or help with managing difficult discussions about royalties (MLMSS 3773 Add on 2040).

Another key event of detailed copyediting for Anderson's novels is for *Taking Shelter*, published by Penguin in 1989 and edited by Susan Hawthorne. These edits show that Anderson was not averse to editorial intervention. Anderson had to explain some of her jokes to Hawthorne (for example, one instance where she had written the text as pig Latin (a joke) and Hawthorne suggested correcting it MLMSS 3773/6/8: 129) and resisted some other changes, but she wrote that she was 'grateful for the detailed work you have done on TAKING SHELTER', and 'happy to have had the chance to make corrections at this early stage' (MLMSS 3773/6/8, 4 January 1989). This demonstrates that Anderson was not against editorial work in principle but the particular case of *Tirra Lirra*'s copyedit.

Tirra Lirra by the River

Tirra Lirra first existed as a short story that won Anderson joint third place in the Captain Cook short story prize (MLMSS 3773 Add on 2040). The original text is not held either in the collection of Anderson's papers at the Mitchell Library or in other papers at the National Library of Australia. As Anderson notes in a draft letter to academic Arleen Sykes dated 23 July (with 83? handwritten in pen on the page), 'Perhaps the short story no longer exists' (MLMSS 3773 Add on 2040). After converting the story into a radio play that aired on the ABC in 1975, Anderson then expanded the work into a novella. Following the publication of *The Commandant*, Anderson returned to the manuscript and on completing the draft, sent it to the Australian arm of her English publisher, who accepted it for publication.

Tirra Lirra is narrated by Nora Porteous, who has returned to her childhood home in Brisbane after the death of her last living relative: her sister Grace. Nora grew up in Brisbane but, eager to leave, moves to Sydney not long after finishing school where she learns dressmaking and marries Colin Porteous. Colin is often described as a kind of unimpressive Sir Lancelot, one of the key players in Alfred Tennyson's poem 'The Lady of Shalott', from which Anderson plucked the title for her novel. Accepting an unfavourable divorce settlement just to get away from her husband, Nora takes a boat to London, having an affair with a fellow passenger on the way: 'He was a middle-aged, squat bodied American,' who 'with five children already ... was delighted by [her] barrenness' (Anderson, 1978: 105). Contrary to his perception of her fertility, Nora falls pregnant and enlists a childhood friend to help her find an abortionist in London. Getting work as a dressmaker, Nora makes it through the war, suffering spells of pleurisy and bronchitis. A client speaks of getting a facelift and Nora is inspired to undergo the surgery herself; only the result is terrible and, on returning to her flat, Nora attempts suicide. After being found and recovering with the help of friends, Nora becomes a costumer at a theatre and finds a new outlet for her talent. She had not planned on returning home but illness and the family house take her back to Brisbane.

The novel is written in first-person present tense with gliding shifts backwards in time as Nora reflects on her childhood, her adolescence, her young life and time in London. She also ruminates on her peers: Olive Partridge who leaves Australia and becomes a successful novelist; and Dorothy Rainbow who stays, marries a local man and later kills almost all her family before killing herself. As with some of Anderson's other books, gay men also make for important characters in her work (Barlow, 2012).

When described in summary, *Tirra Lirra* may seem like a melodramatic work. As critic Roslyn Haynes (1986: 319) argues, 'The novel contains several incidents which invite sensational treatment – Nora's experience at the abortionist's, her attempted suicide, her failed face-lift, Dorothy Rainbow's massacre of her children and subsequent suicide; yet these are related in an almost off-hand way.' Part of the impact of the novel is created by the disconnection between the points of high drama and Nora's almost affectless retelling. It is carefully constructed with parallels to Tennyson's poem and the plight of the woman artist, recurring images of a globe of memory, motifs of tennis playing and the use of colour to maintain a tightly woven, synchronous effect. *Tirra Lirra* is the only one of Anderson's novels to have remained in print from first publication and is still on university and school syllabi.

Editing as a Prompt

Editing is not simply a process of scrawling pen (or adding many tracked changes), it can be much more subtle and operate as a prompt for the author, as was the case for Anderson and one sentence in a letter from her editor. Anderson acknowledges this when she says, in a note accompanying the archive:

> I sent it to Alan Maclean who was a <u>good editor</u>, hoping that he would suggest a way of expanding it rather than asking him to publish it; and he did in fact define the weakness of the U.K. part. I was able to expand this part after a visit to London in 1973. *(MLMSS 3773 Add on 2040)*

The page that follows is the original letter from Maclean dated 2 June 1971, in which he says:

> As far as length goes it is as you know very awkward in form. I believe it is really more a long short story than a short novel, but I don't think that it is satisfactory either way. Looked at as a novel there is a great deal left to the imagination and the whole of the UK experience is only lightly, though marvellously sketched in. Looked at as a very long story the

converse is true and there is too much for the reader to absorb. Your writing has real distinction, insight and clarity and it is just that the shape and structure seems to me to be all wrong.

This is a poor sort of letter which will I am afraid only serve to irritate you. However, it is one of these maddening times when I can think of nothing really constructive to say, at the same time finding only praise for the actual writing.

(MLMSS 3773, Add on 2040)

Maclean's comment about how he cannot think of anything particularly 'constructive' to add is typical of a self-effacing approach to editorial work. This sort of comment is in line with commentary from editors Maxwell Perkins (Berg, 2013: 6) and Beatrice Davis (Kent, 2001: 3) about the role of the editor and the importance of downplaying their contribution, both to maintain the author's sense of control and to ensure that the work is ultimately in line with their intentions.

Since Maclean's letter was, in effect, a rejection, he may have felt the need to be particularly cautious with his wording. However, it would seem that rather than 'irritating' Anderson, she found in his suggestion a path to pursue with an otherwise unpublishable work. In this way, Maclean made an important contribution to the work in that Anderson adopted his suggestion of how to develop it. Notably, Maclean's comments are not prescriptive and are more general suggestions rather than a detailed structural edit. It is what Anderson did with the suggestion that created the award-winning book that *Tirra Lirra* became.

From a commercial perspective, it seems likely that Maclean's suggestion would have had an element of self-interest, since it is a publishing truism that books sell better in markets that feature in the books themselves or, in other words, if the book features more scenes set in England, then it has a greater chance of appealing to English audiences; Maclean is anticipating a English readership for the work and therefore makes a suggestion based on this assessment.

As the interchange demonstrates, the greatest editorial interventions are not always from the person who is professionally engaged as the book's editor.

In Anderson's case it is not a spouse or a close friend but someone whose opinion she trusts and who has been her editor in the past, although he is not taking on that role for her book. Just as Stillinger (1991: 57) notes in his study of *Sister Carrie*, the contributions that lead to editorial development of a work do not always come from those employed to work on it. In the same way as Theodore Dreiser's work was amended in response to commentary from people not employed by the publisher of his book, so Maclean is significant in the history of *Tirra Lirra*, even though he was not the book's editor or publisher. As in the case of a friend or spouse, Maclean's editorial work was provided gratis. For any critique about the commercialism of the publishing process and denigration of the work of major corporations, Maclean's contribution was in the spirit of literary cooperation and while it may have been in his interests to maintain a good relationship with an author whose future work could be profitable, in this instance the time spent reading and the useful criticism he offered were not directly tied to commercial gain for his employer.

Extending the section in London also affords Anderson the opportunity to write more of the relationships between contemporary Australian and English life. At the time the novel was set, when it was still routine for artists to leave Australia for the UK, Nora finds that London is not all that she had imagined of a great city. For instance, Nora is surprised by how difficult it is to get an abortion there, which, Brigid Rooney (2018: 96) says, 'provincializes the great metropolis'. The idea that London would be a sort of artistic haven is also problematised by Nora's discovery that the embroideries she created in Brisbane were significant aesthetic achievements (Anderson, 1978: 92).

One facet that she was able to extend in the London section was the discussion of artistic work as vocation. *Tirra Lirra* is like other works Anderson wrote in that her character has a creative vocation. As in the short story *The Milk*, where the protagonist is an illustrator (1987), Nora initially earns her living working as a seamstress assisting fashion designers in London. Acting as the machinist for other peoples' vision leads to '[t]he privacy of the gratification, the vicariousness of the achievement, and the rationalisation of the whole process [which] tell their own story of the suppression of Nora's identity' (Barry, 1996: 72). The added description of this incarnation of Nora's working life acted as a proxy for her artistic life. Indeed, on hearing of the possibility of the job, Nora says 'my interior eye was assailed by a medley of rich ripping colour, of bright lights and inhabited shadow' (Anderson, 1978: 158). Each of Nora's jobs is important for empowering her at different stages in her life. Her work as a dressmaker gives her independent income when her husband denies her. In London it affords her a living initially, and as a theatre costume maker she finds a job where 'eagerly, after the idleness of Sunday, I returned to my work. I grew to love those big cluttered low-ceilinged rooms, and the memory . . . can still fill me with nostalgia' (160).

Although slight, Maclean's comment on the London section encouraged Anderson to develop these elements of the story that might otherwise have laid dormant. Bedford's review, quoted at the start of this chapter, marks the opening as the section that needed more editorial attention and said that the book would have been better had the standard of editing been equivalent over the entire work. She could not have known that in fact, the middle section was the 'youngest' of the book and that no editor had intervened in the middle or the end of the book at a line level, let alone in terms of developing structure, aside from the one suggestion from Alan Maclean. This also shows the benefits of combining genetic criticism and a focus on professional editing. Rather than simply considering the holographs, iterations and inspirations that contributed to Anderson's drafting, by acknowledging the others who had a role in the production of her book, we can acquire a richer understanding of how the text came to exist.

Editing as Overdetermination

The Title

A title is one of the first elements of a book with which a prospective reader has contact and so it is often a topic of discussion between publishers and authors over the course of the acquisition and editorial process. As demonstrated by Raymond Carver's *What We Talk About When We Talk About Love* – a formulation that has since become hackneyed and reworked for many an essay – titles can have significant lasting cultural impact.

Titles, as Gerard Genette and Marie Maclean (1991: 261) write about paratexts, 'surround . . . and prolong [a work], precisely in order to present it, in usual sense of this verb, but also in its strongest meaning: to make it present, to assure its presence in the world, its "reception" and consumption, in the form, nowadays at least, of a book'. Titles are of critical importance for the publisher because of their concern with reaching a market. It is also a question to which Moretti (2009) devoted attention in his analysis of British novel titles from the mid-eighteenth to the mid-nineteenth century. Moretti found that titles became shorter over this period. Although not based on more recent data, some of his observations still hold; the short titles of the nineteenth century have continued to hold into the present day.

In what must have been an unnerving development for Anderson, she received the contract from Macmillan for a book called *The Crystal Mirror*. The publisher had renamed *Tirra Lirra by the River* without consulting her. As Anderson wrote in response to the contract:

> I have never heard of THE CRYSTAL MIRROR. The title of
> the ms. I sent you is TIRRA LIRRA BY THE RIVER. Has
> someone changed it for me? Or have you got it mixed up with
> another novel? And would you also tell me if you propose to
> publish the two stories (TIRRA LIRRA and THE
> OBEDIENT GIRL in one volume, or only TIRRA LIRRA
> as a short novel. *(MLMSS 3773 Add on 2040, 27 May 1977)*

In a later letter, her editor at Macmillan, Pamela Reid wrote, 'Thank you for your recent letter returning the signed contract for THE CRYSTAL MIRROR' (MLMSS 3773, Add on 2040). Perhaps the strategy at Macmillan was simply to act as if Anderson had accepted the title change until it was too late.

Anderson was determined to keep her original title, offering the opinions of others as evidence for her argument: 'a number of people said they turned [the radio play] on because their curiosity was aroused by the title, and when, in its first genesis as a short story, it won a prize in the Capt. Cook centenary comp., the judges all liked the title' (MLMSS 3773 Add on 2040). Interestingly, in her defence of her original title, Anderson only refers to the comments others made in praise of the title, both commercial and literary judgements, rather than offering her own explanation for its importance; this reticence fits with Anderson's general avoidance of spelling out the subtleties of her work. Her repeated arguments to keep it, however, reinforce how strongly she felt about the need to keep the original title.

The Crystal Mirror would have been an appropriate title for the book, being both thematically tied to the novel and from the same stanza of Tennyson's poem as Anderson's title, a section quoted in the early pages of *Tirra Lirra*: 'From the bank and from the river/ He flash'd into the crystal mirror, "Tirra lirra", by the river/ Sang Sir Lancelot' (Anderson, 1978: 13). This mirror is the device through which the Lady of Shalott is able to view the world, and something that Barry describes as a kind of 'leitmotif' in the book, arguing:

> The novel is in a sense a hall of mirrors: there is the Lady of Shalott's mirror, the 'cheap thick glass' of the window that opens onto the dream landscape of Nora's childhood, the globe of memory inscribed with its 'millions of images', the hand-mirror reflecting the blankness of her identity after her facelift operation, the television screen that reflects a 'shadow' of the real world in her living-room, and the reflections of herself that other people all through her life, have given back to her ('Who does she think <u>she</u> is?'). *(Barry, 1996: 85)*

The mirror is an obvious image for the title but it would have perhaps overemphasised these elements in the book. Instead, Anderson's quite unusual title shifts the focus elsewhere. Critic Roslyn Haynes (1986: 316) contends that the title emphasises the plight of the woman artist and the disappointments of dealing with an ineffectual paramour. The interest scholars have in titles, and Anderson's title in particular, is one of the reasons why this kind of archival research is important to literary studies. By uncovering the requested change and Anderson's resistance, her dedication to her choice of title is clear.

If we think of the suggested title, *The Crystal Mirror*, as an attempt on the part of the publisher to make the book more market-friendly (and in line with more standard titles), then Anderson's resistance is part of a vision for the work that privileges art over the commercial market. Unlike her three previous titles, her insistence on *Tirra Lirra by the River* asserts an ambition for this work aesthetically and in terms of the market. A more unusual title is not simply a question of representing the text to potential readers but it also marks the work as more literary and less commercial; Anderson wants to ensure her work's place in the literary field. It is perhaps also indicative of its genesis in that such a title is not so unusual for a short story, or a radio play for that matter.

Copyediting

While Gordon Lish's editorial strategy with Raymond Carver's work was to remove material, reducing the level of determination, not all editorial suggestions move a work in that direction. In fact, in the interests of clarity or conforming to traditional models, some editors may intervene to add greater determination to a text. This was the case with *Tirra Lirra*'s copyeditor, Pamela Reid. Although the archive includes a letter to Anderson from Susan Nicholls saying, 'I will be looking after your manuscript TIRRA LIRRA BY THE RIVER, as editor and general overseer of its progress through production' (MLMSS 3773 Add on 2040), it seems it was Pamela Reid who edited the book.

There are two kinds of editing that Reid undertook, one at the level of suggested structural changes and the other at the level of a copyedit. Overwhelmingly the changes are for minor amendments such as going from double to single quote marks, an Australian convention, which could be called uncontroversial and related to house style. However, for almost every other change, Anderson wanted to keep the original and rather than simply writing back to reject the changes summarily. There is a draft of her letter, dated 26 August 1977, where she lists each of the edits that she wants retracted and, in many cases, the reason why.

In another letter dated 13 September, Anderson reiterated her concerns:

> On the first of September I wrote to you asking that the alterations made by an editor on the ms. of TIRRA LIRRA BY THE RIVER should be cancelled before it goes to press,

I enclosed three foolscap pages of explanations of each cancellation I asked for, as well as explaining the changes and corrections I made myself.

I have had no acknowledgement of my letter and am rather worried about it. There is a mail strike here, but my other mail from Melbourne is coming through. If you have not already written, would you mind doing so? I would be very pleased to have your assurance that the changes made by your editor will be cancelled. It would be much more expensive and troublesome to make on the proofs.

There is also the title to be decided on. I really can't go past my own title; it is so much better than any other I have thought of. Have you a publication date yet for the book?

(MLMSS 3773/2/2)

Rather than saying she wanted the original reinstated or some other phrasing, Anderson's use of the term 'cancelled' is interesting here. This is a definitive position and not something to be negotiated. Further, she appeals to the editor's sense of frugality, referring to the expense of changing typeset pages. Lastly, her mention both of the title and her ignorance of the publication date show how disempowered and disconnected the author may feel from the publishing process. After nearly a fortnight, she had not had correspondence from Macmillan and was anxious that her book would be published otherwise than she had intended. The language that Anderson uses in her letter, a second letter on the subject since the first went unanswered, is assertive and determined. Compared with Davis and Park's correspondence, for example, it is much more forthright and carries none of the affection or professional admiration.

On the whole, the copyeditor was restrained in her approach to *Tirra Lirra* and her intervention would be equivalent to the work of many contemporary proofreaders. She suggested very little in the way of significant changes, be they at the level of paragraph or sentence, and the changes that she did suggest are, on the whole, easily justified according to editorial convention. An example of a more significant change is Reid's suggestion on a number of occasions to introduce line breaks.

These indicate a greater passage of time; for instance, on page 51, a new paragraph begins 'That night, feeling safe and detached . . .' (MLMSS3773/2/2). From the opening we understand that time has passed from the previous scene and so convention would have it that a section break would be justified. However, as Anderson argues in her letter opposing the changes, 'There is no logic in breaks to indicate a shift in time unless you make one at every shift, in which case this ms. would be a mass of little fragments' (MLMSS3773, Add on 2040). The time shifts Anderson left unmarked by paragraph breaks were part of her vision for the work.

To take one example, Nora's voyage to London is not flagged by a new chapter and so there is a smooth flow between Nora's leaving behind her ex-husband and her affair with the American aboard the boat. This sense of flow is part of Nora's remembering. One of the last Australian scenes is set on the tennis court, and not long after Nora arrives in London. When she is recovering from her abortion at Olive's house, she hears the sounds of tennis and at first considers them a 'remnant of a dream' (Anderson, 1976: 116). The procession of ideas and memories, uninterrupted by the chapter marker that Reid suggested, is indicative of the internal logic to which Anderson referred in her letter. By leading, without a break, from one setting to another, the reader's imagination glides over time and space, just as Nora's does. The insertion of chapter and section breaks makes for a more determined reading experience, narrowing the potential interpretations of a given section and smoothing the prose. This is operating in the opposite way from many other edits; consider Lish's work on Carver where he repeatedly deleted material to offer the reader more room for interpretation (Max, 1998). Anderson seems intent on a work where the text elides time, replicating the experience of memory and the often unexpected shifts in thought that can defy a straightforward chronology.

In every instance where this is a strong section break, the new paragraph is set in the 'present-day' of the novel, that is, Nora at home in Brisbane, age seventy. By only ever having section openings at these points, there is an emphasis on these parts of the narrative and the work that the present is doing. As critic Elaine Barry (1996: 85) notes, 'Much of the effectiveness of the novel rests in the choice of narrative voice – not only the first person, not even the more unusual present tense, but the sense of that present simultaneously lived and observed.' Had Anderson accepted the changes that Reid suggested, the sense of simultaneity would have been disturbed.

This fluid relationship with time plays out in Anderson's other writing from the first of her novels, *An Ordinary Lunacy* (originally published in 1963). To take one marked example, within the space of two pages, Anderson moves from the steps of the courthouse to David Byfield's living room to his mother sitting in a dentist's chair the following day (Anderson, 1987a: 109–10). Moving between events and perspectives slips seamlessly and demonstrates a masterful control of the flow of information and the passage of narrative time. Such prose appears in shorter fiction as well, notably in Anderson's long short story, 'Outdoor Friends', published in *Stories from the Warm Zone and Sydney Stories* (Anderson, 1987b). The story has section breaks but also has scenes that flow from reminiscence to dialogue and back again. Owen, thinking of the woman with whom he is having an affair, shifts from thinking about her approach to feminism, to recalling 'verbatim' a conversation about the anti-nuclear movement and back to his family relationships (173–4). Just as in *Tirra Lirra*, this passage has its own internal logic and although the shifts in time could be marked by a section break, the flow of the memories, analysis and associations make for a rich and engaging work. Time was something Anderson used as a device and a key stylistic component in her fiction. Her editor was not sensitive to it and was working at cross purposes, trying to bring the text in line with a standard style rather than maintaining the author's style.

The archive not only shows Anderson's responses to the edits that she received from Macmillan but a dissenting voice from within Macmillan itself. On 21 September 1977, Anderson's 'editor', Susan Nicholls wrote:

> P.S. I have just received your latest letter and apologise for the delay in acknowledgment. I am able to tell you unofficially that we are moving towards TIRRA LIRRA BY THE RIVER as a title, but no final decision has been made. Also, for your interest, another editor made all the preliminary editorial alterations, almost none of which I agreed with – entre nous. S *(MLMSS add on 2040)*

The note is particularly interesting since Nicholls had claimed in another letter quoted earlier that she would be responsible for *Tirra Lirra* at Macmillan. If it were the case, then why did she allow an edit that she did not agree with to be sent to the author? The note also underlines the fact that all editorial work is subjective and that while Reid may have been following convention in making the recommendations that she did, following those conventions was not necessarily the obvious editorial choice in the case of *Tirra Lirra*.

Editing as Corruption

One of the criticisms levelled at contemporary publishing is that the process of producing books is increasingly rushed (i.e. Clark 2011: n.p.). Consulting the archive shows us that interventions sometimes occur for different reasons. In a letter to Anderson on 27 June 1978, her editor Pamela Reid wrote:

> I do apologise for the punctuation mistakes in this edition. We had a similar problem with another book set by these particular typesetters and we are taking action to ensure that this does not recur. As to the two-line run-on, this was correct at final proofreading stage and is therefore a printer's error. *(MLMSS 3773, Add on 2040)*

From this we understand that there were two kinds of errors in the book: the first introduced by the typesetter and the second introduced at the printing stage. Typesetters' errors should be picked up and corrected at proof stage; for whatever reason, they were not. A printer's error can only be discovered on delivery of the final copies, which, barring a major disaster, will have to be rectified in any subsequent editions, since the only option is a reprint: a costly and time-consuming solution.

The only contemporary reviewer to comment on these errors was Jean Bedford (1978: 41) and her reference to 'printer's errors' seems to be a conscious decision to emphasise the idea that the book was poorly produced, when considered in conjunction with other editorial failings.

However, as mentioned earlier, her assumptions about editing were ill-founded overall.

Aside from printers' errors, there was one other error that has been repeated in a number of critical works but only flagged as incorrect in once instance. In quoting a line from the book, Haynes (1986: 318) notes an error in the original referring to Nora's self-description as a 'student of the French subjunctive tense [sic]'. This should have been 'verb' or 'mood'. Arguably the mistake would be Nora's since the book is told from her perspective and it is plausible that Anderson wrote it incorrectly intentionally, but more likely is that neither author nor editor was conscious of the error.

The effect of these kinds of mistakes is to undermine the confidence of the reader in the publishing company, just as they undermine the confidence of the author who has entrusted their work to editors, typesetters, printers, distributors and booksellers to get their words into the minds of their readers. Such mistakes can have the correlative effect of making readers think that if there are mistakes at the level of words or sentences then there has been insufficient editorial attention to the book. Since *Tirra Lirra* quickly became popular and was reprinted many times, the typographical and printer's errors could be corrected within a fairly short period of time, and so my conjecture is that often when contemporary readers complain that the quality of editing has deteriorated in recent years, their sense of this change is in part because when they read older or successful books, in many instances the edition will be a corrected copy as opposed to the first edition, which is likely to include more errors.

Typesetting errors were not peculiar to *Tirra Lirra*; to take Anderson's next published book, *The Impersonators* (1980), there are many similar mistakes. On pages 174–5 there are three errors in as many paragraphs (immediatelly, neddle, thier) and elsewhere there are typos such as 'Acquarius' (79) and 'eylids' (181). Such mistakes are not symptomatic of a lack of interest in the work; it was the follow-up to Anderson's Miles Franklin winning, best-selling novel. Macmillan would not have neglected editorial procedures on the book. Rather, checks are done by editorial staff who are human and naturally err. The presence of these mistakes shows that equivalent errors in contemporary books are not simply a result of deteriorating standards, but part of a long tradition of mistakes.

These sorts of errors were also not a uniquely Australian problem. In correspondence with her English publisher, Anderson complained of the prevalence of typesetter errors in the proofs for *The Commandant*. George Hardinge replied to Anderson on 24 April 1970:

> I am sorry you were disappointed in the standard of setting … Generally speaking, the standard of computers and setting has not improved in England in the last few years, and I agree that these could have been better. At the same time, having looked at them very closely, I can promise you that this is an average or even above average piece of setting … I am sorry if this is a depressing thought, but I think it is the true position these days.
>
> *(MLMSS 3773 Add on 2040)*

To further compound the problem, these errors were replicated in the American edition of *The Commandant* as Anderson's English agent, Stephanie Townsend, informed her: 'I was absolutely horrified to see that despite what they wrote back, I think in July, they had not after all made the correction' (MLMSS 3773 Add on 2040, 22 October 1976). The importance of these mistakes is that failings in production are not a new phenomenon, and Anderson suffered from human error in a number of her books.

Conclusion

The edits, both from Alan Maclean and Pamela Reid, demonstrate the push and pull of editorial work and complicate the narrative about editorial processes. In writing about editing the focus is usually on single author–editor studies (c.f. Groenland, 2019) and in genetic criticism the focus usually rests on the individual author. Textual critic Stillinger goes some way to acknowledge that there are multiple players though in a limited fashion.[15] In professional editing the work at different phases of the process determines the kinds of edits that they suggest, and an author's response to them. Importantly, different editors often are working with different ends in

[15] See, for example, Stillinger on Dreiser and *Sister Carrie* discussed in Section 3.

mind, in part because of their interpretations of the work and anticipations of the market. Maclean, working in the UK, naturally would have had an English audience in mind. Reed, working in Australia, potentially with experience working on more trade rather than literary titles, would have imagined a different reader. The book ultimately belongs to the author – after all, it is their name on the spine – and so Anderson's objections both to the title and the editorial changes were respected.

What makes this study so useful is the way in which it demonstrates that editing is a multivalent process and that a published work is the result of multiple contributions.

By examining both the helpful suggestions of Alan Maclean and the problematic suggestions of Pamela Reid, we can follow the practical and aesthetic movements of the editing process and trace the acts of art that led to the celebrated novel *Tirra Lirra by the River*.

Conclusion

The case studies in this Element begin to describe some of the extraordinary range that editorial work covers, from minor suggestions to huge excisions. Editing is a dynamic enterprise, a process of negotiation and collaboration, and, while there is a finished product at the end, it is not simply a straightforward, replicable process. Each case involves different kinds of decision-making as the result of different kinds of pressures and guiding influences. By looking at these edits in detail, we are moving away from a narrow idea about what editorial work is, that edits must always be private, invisible and undiscussed, and through to an understanding of the contributions that editors make as part of the book publishing process, regardless of whether their interventions are intentional, thoughtful and helpful, or whether they are unexpected by-products, inhibitions or mis-readings of the submitted manuscripts.

When we talk about editorial intervention, it is not simply the outlier cases that call for our attention. The 'ordinary' work of editing and the myriad forces that impact that work are just as illuminating, both for students and scholars of editing, and for literary studies more broadly. When we pay attention to the changes in creative texts as they pass through the publication process, we garner important information about social and cultural norms, about representation, gatekeeping and the relationships between individual actors and larger interests on the literary field. Focusing on professional editing (as distinct from the work of textual editors, and scholars of textual editing) as a part of the creative process to be recognised and considered in its own right, a process that has notable and demonstrable effects on the text, marks a shift from scholarship that has gone before in the textual editing space and builds out some cases studies for what Greenberg worked to describe in *A Poetics of Editing*.

Where textual editing is useful is in the idea of 'versions', which came 'into prominence in the 1970s [and is] based on the idea that every separate version of a work has its own legitimacy' (Stillinger, 1991: 197–8). This theory dovetails with Greenberg's (2018: 14) emphasis on the importance of thinking about editing as a *process*, putting a work 'into a context that helps to deliver the meaning and significance of the work to its readers.

Considering the interventions of professional editing in different versions of a text means we are not simply concerned with determining an author's final intentions, as is the preoccupation of textual editing scholars (Stillinger, 1991: 195), or separating out which individual made which change/correction/corruption, but the methodology also generates a way to understand the literary field from the texts that result in the published work: a way to separate a text into some genetic parts in order to analyse the intentions, pressures and negotiations that led to the published product and a way to understand the broader social and literary conditions in which the text was formed, modified and released. Examining the 'social and an institutional event' of publishing a book, as McGann (1983: 100) describes literary production, as opposed to the fixation on the individual author, we can think about how professional editing is contributing to different versions of a work and is not simply what some textual editors would call 'corruption' (McGann, 1983: 21). Further, the contributions made by individuals to the production of the book reveal important information about social conditions, interpersonal dynamics, aesthetic trends and commercial forces.

Literary studies scholars are like textual editors in that they have what McGann (1983: 122) calls '[a] hypnotic fascination with the isolated author [which] has served to foster an overdetermined concept of authorship, but (reciprocally) an underdetermined concept of literary work'. For the most part, when writing about a work, perhaps because of the sake of timeliness and in other cases because of practicalities, these scholars do not focus on the means of production and the individuals involved with the drafting and publication process. What the case studies in this Element show is the different ways in which analysing the editing reveals crucial information about the text, in terms of how it came to be in its published form, which embodied agents contributed to the text and how their interpretations of social norms impact on the changes the work undergoes. The methodology offers a way to answer questions that scholars ask about the work in a more definitive fashion than conjecture on the basis of interpretation.

What it teaches students of editing is just what the implications of their future work can be. With trade publishers not offering the same kind of apprenticeships as in the past and the difficulty of junior staff getting access to work as an editor, study of the kind that I have undertaken here gives an invaluable insight into the kinds of negotiations that editors engage in; what it means to apply rules inappropriately or in a ham-fisted way, in the case of Jessica Anderson's copyeditor, and how editors can assist authors to realise not just their vision for a work but also open up possibilities for a work that perhaps the author themselves had not imagined, in the case of Alan Maclean. We have seen how editors can underestimate an audience, as in the case of *Swords and Crowns and Rings*, or how they can help with navigating the expectations of cultural representation, as in the case of *Multiple Effects of Rainshadow*. This demonstrates, in detail, and in a practical way, how editing operates and what the function of editing really is, using whole books as examples, not just anecdotes, as is the case in some existing discussions of editing. While these anecdotes serve a purpose, they do not (and cannot) give a student of editing an understanding of how editing operates. It is particularly important that these case studies are not outliers. It is also important that these are studies of female authors and (largely) female editors since, to date, the focus in studies of editing has been on male authors and editors. Since publishing as an industry, in Western countries, has been historically dominated by those of majority backgrounds with a certain level of financial and social privilege, it will take study on more contemporary texts to bring to light the work of editors of colour, First Nations and migrant editors. It will also involve a different methodology, since I have consulted paper archives for this study.

By foregrounding the different versions of a manuscript before it is published, and acknowledging the different contributions (or interruptions) of professional editors, we gain fascinating, often unexpected insights into the processes of textual production, the priorities of the author, the anticipated marketplaces, and social aesthetic and commercial pressures on a given text. It is to our detriment to leave author's, editor's and publisher's archives unexamined, given the extraordinary treasures they contain for scholars and editors alike.

Appendix: Ngram of the Use of 'Murri'

Google Books Ngram Viewer

murri

1800 - 2019 ▾   English (2019) ▾   Case-Insensitive   Smoothing ▾

×   ?

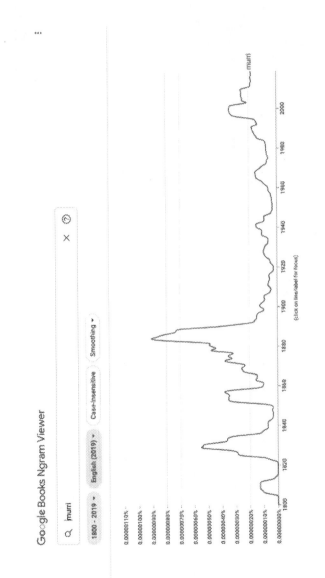

0.000000110% ⌐
0.000000100% ⌐
0.000000090% ⌐
0.000000080% ⌐
0.000000070% ⌐
0.000000060% ⌐
0.000000050% ⌐
0.000000040% ⌐
0.000000030% ⌐
0.000000020% ⌐
0.000000010% ⌐
0.000000000% ⌐

1800   1820   1840   1860   1880   1900   1920   1940   1960   1980   2000

(click on line/label for focus)

murri

References

Adelaide, Debra. 1996. 'Northern Disclosure'. *Sydney Morning Herald*, 28 September, sec. Spectrum.

Anderson, Jessica. 1978. *Tirra Lirra by the River*. South Melbourne: Macmillan.

1980. *The Impersonators*. South Melbourne: Macmillan.

1987a. *An Ordinary Lunacy*. Ringwood, Vic.: Penguin Books.

1987b. *Stories from the Warm Zone and Sydney Stories*. Ringwood, Vic.: Penguin Books.

n.d. 'Papers'. Mitchell Library, SLNSW.

Astley, Thea. 1972. *The Acolyte*. Sydney: Angus and Robertson.

1978. *Being a Queenslander*. Sydney: The Wentworth Press.

1982. *An Item from the Late News*. St Lucia, Qld: University of Queensland Press.

1985. *Beachmasters*. Ringwood, Vic.: Penguin Books.

1987. *It's Raining in Mango: Pictures from the Family Album*. Ringwood, Vic.: Viking.

1988. *The Well Dressed Explorer*. Ringwood, Vic.: Penguin.

1999. *Drylands: A Book for the World's Last Reader*. Ringwood, Vic.: Viking.

2012. *Girl with a Monkey*. Crows Nest, NSW: Allen & Unwin House of Books.

2018a. *The Multiple Effects of Rainshadow*. Text Classics. Melbourne: Text Publishing.

2018b. *A Kindness Cup*. Melbourne: Text Publishing.

n.d. 'Papers'. Fryer Library.

Athill, Diana. 2011. *Stet*. London: Granta.

Barker, Anthony, and Vic. Society of Editors (Melbourne). 1991. *One of the First and One of the Finest: Beatrice Davis, Book Editor*. Carlton, Vic.: Society of Editors (Vic.).

Barlow, Damien. 2012. 'The Queerness of Jessica Anderson's Fiction'. *Southerly* 72(1): 136–52.

Barry, Elaine. 1996. *Fabricating the Self: The Fictions of Jessica Anderson*. New rev. ed. UQP Studies in Australian Literature. St Lucia, Qld: University of Queensland Press.

Bedford, Jean. 1978. 'Expatriate's Return Home'. *The National Times*, 9 September.

Berg, A. Scott. 2013. *Max Perkins: Editor of Genius*. London: Simon & Schuster.

Bourdieu, Pierre, and Randal Johnson. 1993. *The Field of Cultural Production: Essays on Art and Literature*. New York: Columbia University Press.

Brett, Mandy. 2011. 'Stet by Me: Thoughts on Editing Fiction'. *Meanjin*. https://meanjin.com.au/essays/stet-by-me-thoughts-on-editing-fiction/

Chetwynd, Ali, Joanna Freer and Georgios Maragos, eds. 2018. *Thomas Pynchon, Sex, and Gender*. Athens: The University of Georgia Press.

Clark, Alex. 2011. 'The Lost Art of Editing'. *The Guardian*, 12 February. www.theguardian.com/books/2011/feb/11/lost-art-editing-books-publishing.

Conley, David. 1986. 'Astley Makes the Read Hard Work'. *Gold Coast Bulletin*. March. Fryer.

Cosic, Miriam. 2016. 'How an Editor Brings the Writer's Work Squalling into the World'. *Australian Financial Review Magazine*, 24 February. www.afr.com/life-and-luxury/anna-funder-christos-tsiolkas-tim-flannery-on-the-editorwriter-relationship-20160112-gm49x0.

Dale, Leigh. 2008. Colonial History and Post-colonial Fiction: The Writing of Thea Astley. In Susan Sheridan and Paul Genoni (eds.), *Thea Astley's Fictional Worlds*. Newcastle upon Tyne: Cambridge Scholars.

n.d. 'Colonial History and Post-Colonial Fiction: The Writing of Thea Astley'. *Australian Literary Studies* 19(1): 21–30.

Davis, Beatrice. n.d. 'Papers'. Mitchell Library, SLNSW.

Davis, Lennard J. 2013. *The Disability Studies Reader*. 4th ed. New York: Routledge.

Dever, Maryanne, Ann Vickery and Sally Newman. 2009. *The Intimate Archive: Journeys through Private Papers*. Canberra: National Library of Australia.

Dixon, Robert M. W., W. S. Ramson and Mandy Thomas. 1992. *Australian Aboriginal Words in English: Their Origin and Meaning*. New York: Oxford University Press.

Einsohn, Amy, and Marilyn Schwartz. 2019. *The Copyeditor's Handbook: A Guide for Book Publishing and Corporate Communications*. 4th ed. Oakland: University of California Press.

Ellison, Jennifer, ed. 1986. *Rooms of Their Own*. Ringwood, Vic.: Penguin.

English, James. 2010. 'Everywhere and Nowhere: The Sociology of Literature After "the Sociology of Literature"'. *New Literary History* 41(2): v–xxiii.

Flann, Elizabeth, Beryl Hill and Lan Wang. 2014. *The Australian Editing Handbook*. 3rd ed. Milton, Qld: John Wiley & Sons.

Foley, Abram. 2021. *The Editor Function: Literary Publishing in Postwar America*. Minneapolis: University of Minnesota Press.

Garner, Helen. 1982. 'In the Tradition of Wake in Fright'. *National Times*, 17 October.

Genette, Gerard, and Marie Maclean. 1991. 'Introduction to the Paratext'. *New Literary History* 22(2): 261.

Gilbert, Pam. 1988. *Coming Out from Under: Contemporary Australian Women Writers*. Australian Literary Heritage. London: Pandora.

Ginna, Peter, ed. 2017. *What Editors Do: The Art, Craft, and Business of Book Editing*. Chicago Guides to Writing, Editing, and Publishing. Chicago: University of Chicago Press.

Gottlieb, Robert. 2016. *Avid Reader: A Life*. 1st ed. New York: Farrar, Straus and Giroux.

Greaves, Jill. 1996. '"The Craft So Long to Learn": Ruth Park's Story of Ruth Park'. *Australian Literary Studies* 17(3): 244–53.

Greenberg, Susan. 2015. *Editors Talk about Editing: Insights for Readers, Writers and Publishers*. Mass Communication and Journalism 11. New York: Peter Lang.

   2018. *A Poetics of Editing*. 1st ed. Cham: Palgrave Macmillan.

Grenville, Kate, and Sue Woolfe. 2001. *Making Stories: How Ten Australian Novels Were Written*. Crows Nest, NSW: Allen & Unwin.

Groenland, Tim. 2019. *Art of Editing: Raymond Carver and David Foster Wallace*. New York: Bloomsbury Academic USA.

Gross, Gerald, ed. 1993. *Editors on Editing: What Writers Need to Know about What Editors Do*. 3rd ed. New York: Grove Press.

Grossman, Michele. 2013. *Entangled Subjects: Indigenous/Australian Cross-Cultures of Talk, Text, and Modernity*. Cross/Cultures 158. Amsterdam: Rodopi.

Hay, Louis. 2014. 'Psychoanalytic Reading and the Avant-Texte'. In Jed Deppman, Daniel Ferrer, and Michael Groden (eds.), *Genetic Criticism: Texts and Avant-Textes*, *Material Texts*. Philadelphia: University of Pennsylvania Press: 17–27.

Haynes, Roslynn. 1986. 'Art as Reflection in Jessica Anderson's *Tirra Lirra by the River*'. *Australian Literary Studies* 12(3): 316–23.Heiss, Anita. 2003. *Dhuuluu-yala, To Talk Straight: Publishing Indigenous Literature*. Canberra: Aboriginal Studies Press.

Herman, Luc, and John M. Krafft. 2007. 'Fast Learner: The Typescript of Pynchon's V. at the Harry Ransom Center in Austin'. *Texas Studies in Literature and Language* 49(1): 1–20.

   2015. 'Monkey Business: The Chapter "Millennium" Removed from an Early Version of *V*'. In Paolo Simonetti and Umberto Rossi (eds.),

Dream Tonight of Peacock Tails: Essays on the Fiftieth Anniversary of Thomas Pynchon's V. Newcastle upon Tyne: Cambridge Scholars Publishing, 2015: 13–30.

    2018. 'Pynchon and Gender: A View from the Typescript of *V*'. In Ali Chetwynd, Joanna Freer, and Georgios Maragos (eds.), T*homas Pynchon, Sex, and Gender*. Athens: University of Georgia Press.

Irvine, Dean. 2016. *Editing Modernity: Women and Little-Magazine Cultures in Canada, 1916–1956.* Toronto: University of Toronto Press.

Jones, Jennifer. 2009. *Black Writers, White Editors: Episodes of Collaboration and Compromise in Australian Publishing History*. North Melbourne: Australian Scholarly Publishing.

Jordan, Ray. 1978. 'A Testimony to One of Life's Heroes'. *The West Australian*, 28 November.

Kent, Jacqueline. 2001. *A Certain Style: Beatrice Davis, a Literary Life*. Camberwell, Vic.: Penguin Books.

Koch, Christopher. 2012. *The Year of Living Dangerously*. Pymble, NSW: HarperCollins Australia.

Koestenbaum, Wayne. 1989. *Double Talk: The Erotics of Male Literary Collaboration*. New York: Routledge.

Lamb, Karen. 2015. *Thea Astley: Inventing Her Own Weather*. St Lucia, Qld: University of Queensland Press.

Leane, Jeanine. 2014. 'Tracking Our Country in Settler Literature'. *Journal of the Association for the Study of Australian Literature*. 14 March.

Lever, Susan. 2008. 'Changing Times, Changing Stories'. In Susan Sheridan and Paul Genomi (eds.). *Thea Astley's Fictional Worlds*. Newcastle upon Tyne: Cambridge Scholars Publishing: 126–34.

Mackenzie, Janet. 2011. *The Editor's Companion*. 2nd ed. Port Melbourne, Vic.: Cambridge University Press.

Marek, Jayne E. 1995. *Women Editing Modernism: 'Little' Magazines & Literary History*. Lexington: University Press of Kentucky.

Max, D. T. 1998. 'The Carver Chronicles'. *New York Times Magazine*, 9 August. Proquest.

McCormack, Thomas. 2006. *The Fiction Editor, the Novel, and the Novelist*. 2nd ed. Philadelphia: Paul Dry Books.

McGann, Jerome J. 1983. *A Critique of Modern Textual Criticism*. Chicago: University of Chicago Press.

1991. *The Textual Condition*. Princeton Studies in Culture/Power/History. Princeton, NJ: Princeton University Press.

McRobbie, Diana. 1983. 'Don't Let the Flaws Stop You Reading'. *Gold Coast Bulletin*, 2 January.

Miner, Valerie. 1988. 'The Brilliant Career of Thea Astley'. *Los Angeles Times*, 7 August.

Mitchell, David, and Sharon Snyder. 2013. Narrative Prosthesis. In Lennard J. David (ed.), *The Disability Studies Reader*, 4th ed. New York: Routledge: 222–35.

Moretti, Franco. 2009. 'Style Inc., Reflections on Seven Thousand Titles (British Novels 1740–1850)'. *Critical Inquiry* 36(1): 134–58.

Munro, Craig. 2021. *Literary Lion Tamers: Book Editors Who Made Publishing History*. Brunswick, Vic.: Scribe.

Park, Ruth. 1955. *Pink Flannel*. Sydney: Angus & Robertson.

2009. *The Harp in the South Trilogy*. Camberwell, Vic.: Penguin Group Australia.

2012. *Swords and Crowns and Rings*. Text Classics. Melbourne: Text Publishing.

2019a. *A Fence Around the Cuckoo*. Text Classics. Melbourne: Text Publishing.

2019b. *Fishing in the Styx*. Text Classics. Melbourne: Text Publishing.

n.d. 'Papers'. Mitchell Library, SLNSW.

Perkins, Elizabeth. 1992. 'Violence and Intellect: Thea Astley's Prose Style'. *Australian Book Review*, no. 144 (September).

Prior, Renarta. 1993. *Straight from the Yudaman's Mouth: The Life Story of Peter Prior: Before, during, and after the Robert Curry Days, Never Told Before*. Townsville, Qld: Dept. of History & Politics, James Cook University.

Riddell, Elizabeth. 1977. 'The Lord of the Gold and Rings'. *The Australian, Weekend Magazine*, 5 November.

Rodoreda, Geoff. 2018. *The Mabo Turn in Australian Fiction*. Australian Studies: Interdisciplinary Perspectives 1. Oxford: Peter Lang.

Rooney, Brigid. 2018. *Suburban Space, the Novel and Australian Modernity*. London: Anthem Press.

Sheridan, Susan. 2011. 'Historical Novels Challenging the National Story'. *History Australia* 8(2): 7–20.

——— 2016. *The Fiction of Thea Astley*. Cambria Australian Literature Series. Amherst, NY: Cambria Press.

Shoemaker, Adam. 1989. *Black Words, White Page: Aboriginal Literature, 1929–1988*. UQP Studies in Australian Literature. St Lucia, Qld: University of Queensland Press.

Simonetti, Paolo, and Umberto Rossi, eds. 2015. *Dream Tonight of Peacock Tails: Essays on the 50th Anniversary of Thomas Pynchon's V*. Newcastle upon Tyne: Cambridge Scholars Publishing.

Stillinger, Jack. 1991. *Multiple Authorship and the Myth of Solitary Genius*. New York: Oxford University Press.

Sullivan, Hannah. 2013. *The Work of Revision*. Cambridge, MA: Harvard University Press.

Taylor, Cheryl. 2009. '"This Fiction, It Don't Go Away": Narrative as an Index to Palm Island's Past and Present'. *Queensland Review* 16(1): 35–67.

——— 2021. 'The Genesis of Thea Astley's *Multiple Effects of Rainshadow*'. *Journal of the Association for the Study of Australian Literature [Online]* 21(1): n.p.

Throsby, David, Jan Zwar and Callum Morgan. 2017. 'Reading the Reader: A Survey of Australian Reading Habits'. Macquarie University. www.businessandeconomics.mq.edu.au/__data/assets/pdf_file/0018/528030/FinalFinalReaders-Report-24-05-17-final.pdf.

Throsby, David, Jan Zwar, Tom Longden and Paul Crosby. 2015. *The Australian Book Industry : Authors, Publishers and Readers in a Time of Change*. Sydney: Macquarie University. www.businessandeconomics.mq.edu.au/our_departments/Economics/econ_research/reach_network/book_project/about.

Togo, Christine, dir. 1997. *Straight from the Yudaman's Mouth*. Film. Townsville, Qld: Big Eye Productions.

'Tribute to Beatrice Davis'. 1974. Manuscript. MLMSS 2808.

Triesman, Deborah. n.d. 'The New Yorker Fiction Podcast'. www.newyorker.com/podcast/fiction/anne-enright-reads-frank-oconnor.

Van Toorn, Penelope. 2006. *Writing Never Arrives Naked: Early Aboriginal Cultures of Writing in Australia*. Canberra: Aboriginal Studies Press.

Venuti, Lawrence. 2010. 'Translation, Empiricism, Ethics'. *Profession*: 72–81.

Walker, Shirley. 2009. 'Bitter Fruit: Ruth Park's Trilogy'. *Australian Book Review* 313 (August): 25–26.

Wrathall, Andrew. 2018. 'For Love or Money: Employment in the Australian Publishing Industry in 2018'. *Books and Publishing* (November). www.booksandpublishing.com.au/articles/2018/11/21/118475/for-love-or-money-analysing-the-employment-survey/.

Acknowledgments

The author would like to acknowledge Kemalde Pty Ltd c/- Tim Curnow, literary agent and consultant, Sydney for access to Ruth Park's archive, held at the Mitchell Library at the State Library of New South Wales.

Thanks to the Fryer Library at the University of Queensland; the Rae and George Hammer Memorial fellowship supported time with and access to Thea Astley's archive.

Thanks to Dr Julieanne Lamond at the Australian National University and series editor Dr Susan Greenberg whose feedback was invaluable, and thanks to David and Arthur Henley for putting up with me.

Cambridge Elements ≡

Publishing and Book Culture

SERIES EDITOR

Samantha Rayner
University College London

Samantha Rayner is Professor of Publishing and Book Cultures at UCL. She is also Director of UCL's Centre for Publishing, co-Director of the Bloomsbury CHAPTER (Communication History, Authorship, Publishing, Textual Editing and Reading) and co-Chair of the Bookselling Research Network.

ASSOCIATE EDITOR

Leah Tether
University of Bristol

Leah Tether is Professor of Medieval Literature and Publishing at the University of Bristol. With an academic background in medieval French and English literature and a professional background in trade publishing, Leah has combined her expertise and developed an international research profile in book and publishing history from manuscript to digital.

About the Series

This series aims to fill the demand for easily accessible, quality texts available for teaching and research in the diverse and dynamic fields of Publishing and Book Culture. Rigorously researched and peer-reviewed Elements will be published under themes, or 'Gatherings'. These Elements should be the first check point for researchers or students working on that area of publishing and book trade history and practice: we hope that, situated so logically at Cambridge University Press, where academic publishing in the UK began, it will develop to create an unrivalled space where these histories and practices can be investigated and preserved.

Cambridge Elements ☰

Publishing and Book Culture

Editors and Editing

Gathering Editor: Susan Greenberg

Susan Greenberg is Senior Lecturer in the University of
Roehampton's School of Humanities and Social Sciences. She is
also convener of the MA Publishing and Publisher of the
School's in-house imprint, Fincham Press. Her last book,
A Poetics of Editing (2018), makes a case for a new field of
Editing Studies.

Printed in the United States
by Baker & Taylor Publisher Services